Title Page

Election Countdown 2020: A Predictive Analysis

2021 Edition with Result

Copyright by Alan Sewell

First publication date: 04/06/2019

Revision: 04/05/2021

Print ISBN: 978-1-7339220-0-5

Feedback: alsnewideas@gmail.com

Other books by Alan Sewell   https://www.amazon.com/Alan-Sewell/e/B00557PQDY

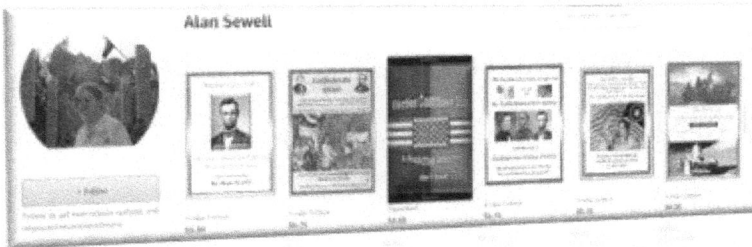

Contents

Election Result

This is a post-election (April 5, 2021) follow-up to **Election Countdown 2020**, first published in April 2019. I thought the predictive analysis of the trends at that time would have value in predicting the election outcome a year and a half in the future. Amazon's #1 ranked Hall of Fame reviewer wrote:

- *What I do very much appreciate is the author's obvious deep investigation and research into election politics.... I do most highly recommend reading **"Election Countdown 2020,"** even while I so strenuously disagree with his prediction... Certainly, this book will advance more than a few of us into discussing America's future and the need to rebuild American governance...*

In April 2019 we were sharply divided on whether Trump's turbulent presidency should be continued. The turmoil accelerated during the next eighteen months. In August 2020, a YouTube wag remarked: "The 2020s are the longest decade I've ever lived, and we're only two-thirds of the first year into it!" At the peak of the rioting, and with fears of a contested election looming, we came as close to having an all-out civil war at least since the 1960s, or maybe even as far back as *the* Civil War of 1861-1865.

I expected this would be the great showdown between the Republican Populist Right and the Democratic Progressive Left, that would set our political direction for the rest of the century.

Either Trump would be confirmed to lead the country in a populist, nationalist, anti-Globalist direction, or the Democratic Progressives would lead us into a return of the liberal internationalist New Deal.

Now, five months after the election, it is still difficult to analyze. The election wasn't a "Blue Wave" because the Republicans won 14 seats in the House of Representatives. They went on to lose the two Georgia Senate Seats in runoffs, but these were weak Republican Establishment candidates not aligned with Trump's populist brand. Nevertheless, the Democrats took these victories to be their green light to enact a Progressive agenda of open borders, higher taxes, and the Green New Deal.

Biden seemed an unlikely Progressive. As a candidate, he appeared to favor a return to the center, by rolling the political clock backward --- past Donald Trump, past Barack Obama, past George W. Bush, and maybe all the way back to Bill Clinton's administration. He is unique as the only President elected from his "Silent Generation," born between 1928 and 1945, wedged in between the Greatest Generation that primarily fought World War II and the Baby Boomers born after the war. The heyday of the Silent Generation as young up-and-comers was the 1950s. In 1951, *Time Magazine* characterized them:

The most startling fact about the younger generation is its silence. With some rare exceptions, youth is nowhere near the rostrum. By comparison with the Flaming Youth of their fathers

& mothers, today's younger generation is a still, small flame. It does not issue manifestoes, make speeches or carry posters. It has been called the "Silent Generation."

They were known as "men in the gray flannel suits" who worked as corporation drones, living comfortably but anonymously, until they retired at 65 with a gold watch. They valued conformity, consensus building, and teamwork. That generation is now ancient. Biden was born in November 1942. He was in his crib when Americans stormed ashore at Normandy and raised the flag over Iwo Jima. Although his generation is unheralded in its quiet demeanor of living in the shadows of its flamboyant Greatest Generation fathers and Boomer children, its last living survivors, including Biden, should not be underestimated.

I have some affinity for Biden. I knew of his Senate record in 2000, when Colombia, the birth country of my wife and son, was teetering on the brink of joining Venezuela and Cuba in the terminal decay of communism. President Clinton and most Congressional Republicans wanted to provide U.S. military and economic aid to help Colombia's government defeat communist guerillas and cocaine cartels. Most Congressional Democrats, wary of becoming involved in another country's internal struggles, opposed the plan. Biden went to Colombia to see for himself. "We've got to get those people some help," he told his fellow Democrats. Plan Colombia was approved. The military, economic, and morale boost from the United States saved that country, and hence my family.

I also appreciated Biden's gentlemanly debate with vice presidential candidate Sarah Palin in 2008. And his magnificent speech at the Democratic National Convention in 2012 when he said, "Osama Bin Laden is dead and General Motors is alive!" I felt he was severely underrated, despite blunders such as plagiarizing other politicians' speeches almost word for word, that derailed his prior campaigns. Despite voting Republican since 1980, I voted for and campaigned for Obama and Biden in 2012. In 2014 I wrote Biden, suggesting that he run for President in 2016. I did not believe Ms. Clinton could be elected president, and I did not think the Republicans would nominate a candidate I could vote for.

When Trump unexpectedly won the Republican nomination, I voted for him in 2016. I felt he was correct in controlling the border, confronting China on trade deficits and stealing our intellectual property, and shaking up the self-serving Washington Establishment bureaucracy. I voted to re-elect him in 2020. However, I am pledged to give Biden a fair hearing by refraining from criticizing him for at least his first year. I may not criticize him at all if his administration proves sound.

Was the Election "Stolen?"

Was this election "stolen" as Trump and many in his camp allege? In my view, it wasn't "stolen" because it followed the legal procedures established by the Constitution and the state and local courts. Trump's defeat and Biden's victory happened because of several factors working in combination:

First, Trump voters must admit that Trump defeated himself. Successful coaches don't make excuses for losing. They don't say: "We played an away game during a rainstorm that hurt our passing game, and the referees were against us." Even if the coach believes all that is true, he / she says: "Let's look at ourselves. We lost it. What do we need to do to improve?"

I do think Covid, mail-in ballots, and riots defeated Trump, but only in combination with his inability to make the election appear larger than himself. He lost for the same reason Ms. Clinton did in 2016, by making himself look smaller than life. In the final months of the campaign, he talked little about fulfilling his campaign promises of reducing the trade deficit with China and controlling the border with Mexico, let alone his vision for a second term. He got into a one-on-one personal dual with his challenger, always foolish for an incumbent president, and was worsted by Biden. His first debate was perhaps the worst ever by an incumbent president. I'm wondering if Covid deranged his mind.

He also fell into the trap of being baited by the Democrats in the media, the way they ridicule and mock all Republican presidents and mischaracterize their motives and integrity (which the Republican media also does with Democrats). Their allegations of Russian Collusion were concocted by Democrat operatives in the intelligence agencies and Department of Justice and broadcast incessantly by the Liberal media, while they covered up the real collusions, including the funding of the Biden family by persons associated with the governments of Russia and China. Trump could have countered that criticism, simply by saying that the Mueller Commission found no evidence of collusion. But, like President Nixon before him, he became so obsessed with hating his enemies affiliated with Democrats (he also lost no time letting it be known that he was not fond of many Republicans) that he no longer appeared worthy of holding the office of President.

Even so, *The Washington Post* noted on November 18 that in one critical way the election was closer than in 2016:

https://www.washingtonpost.com/opinions/2020/11/18/how-2020-election-was-closer-than-2016/

Opinion: We came much closer to an election catastrophe than many realize

The 2020 election was, in one critical way, even closer than 2016....here are the margins by which Biden won three critical states, as of Wednesday morning:

Arizona: 10,457

Georgia: 14,028

Wisconsin: 20,565

…. the bullet we just dodged, all because of 45,000 votes.

But if Trump had managed to get those 45,000 votes, he would have won 37 more electoral votes, making the electoral college a 269-to-269 tie. Under the Constitution, the election would have then been decided by the House of Representatives, with each state delegation getting just one vote. Even though Democrats have a majority in the House, more state delegations have Republican majorities. Trump would have been reelected.

The unsolicited mail-out / mail-in ballots prompted by the Covid pandemic may have allowed the Democrats to do more "harvesting" of ballots filled in by party activists on behalf of other people than would have occurred if in-person voting had predominated as in prior elections. Perhaps there was more "adjudication" of dubious mail-in ballots in Democrat-run precincts that favored Biden than would have been permitted under the rules of in-person voting.

Another view is that Biden simply outpolled Trump fair and square in the legal vote. Biden is credited with 51.3% of the national popular vote, an improvement of 3.1% over Ms.

Clinton's 48.2% in 2016. Trump also increased his percentage of the national vote to 46.9% in 2020, an improvement of .8% from his 46.1% in 2016. Biden improved the Democrat margin by nearly 4 to 1 (3.1% to .8%).

How was it possible for both candidates to improve their percentage of the popular vote? It's because 5.7% of the 2016 vote went to the Libertarian and Green parties. Their vote diminished to 1.8% in 2020. Biden and Trump split the other 3.9%, with Biden getting the lion's share, especially in some critical suburban counties in states like Georgia. On the other hand, Trump enormously improved his vote in some Hispanic-heavy areas like Miami-Dade in Florida and the Rio Grande valley in Texas.

It was an astounding turnout for both candidates, ginned up by extraordinary passion in such a decisive election combined with extraordinary circumstances of unsolicited mail-out / mail-in ballots. Whereas Trump increased his vote count by 11 million over 2016, Biden increased his by 14 million over Ms. Clinton. The electoral vote count is almost an exact reversal of the 2016 result with Biden winning the same 306 that Trump won then.

A microcosm of the election is Florida vs. Georgia, two seemingly similar Sunbelt states. Why did Trump win Florida by a significantly improved 51.2% to Biden's 47.9% in 2020 compared to 49.1% vs. Ms. Clinton's 47.8% in 2016? It's mainly because he improved his margins in heavily Latino counties like Miami-Dade by winning 46% in 2020 vs. 34% in 2016. Trump's campaign succeeded spectacularly well in our third largest state, which has a tradition of razor-thin election margins.

Why did Trump lose in Georgia with 49.3% to Biden's 49.5%? It's partly because Florida is 26% Hispanic, while Georgia is only 10%. There weren't enough Hispanics in Georgia for Trump's gains among that group to be decisive. The proportion of African American voters is 30% in Georgia vs. 16% in Florida, a constituency that voted around 88% Democratic. Trump also decisively lost Atlanta's prosperous suburban counties of Cobb and Gwinnett. They have been trending Democratic as most other urban areas have. If there is one dominant reason for Trump losing Georgia, it is to be found in those two counties. Possibly, a factor is that Florida had more rigid voting requirements than Georgia in requiring I.D.'s to be shown to obtain ballots, but I am equally satisfied that the differing demographics between the two states accounted for the difference in outcomes.

I've also looked at some midsize Republican-leaning counties like Kent (Grand Rapids) in Michigan. Trump's 2020 vote in Kent County was 46%, down from 48.3% in 2016. In Erie County, Pennsylvania, Trump's margin of 48.8% was the same as in 2016, while Biden improved to 49.8% from Ms. Clinton's 46.8%. It seems that some Democrats who couldn't vote for Ms. Clinton in 2016 decided that Biden was acceptable. It's remarkable that Trump increased his vote in Wayne County (Detroit) to 30.7% in 2020 from 29.5% in 2016, and to 18.2% in

Philadelphia in 2020 from 15.5% in 2016. He made gains in those heavily African American areas, but not enough to offset his losses elsewhere.

In that regard I believe the death of George Floyd in police custody may have influenced the election toward Biden's victory. It is my opinion that the Democratic mayors and governors of several cities and states allowed rioting to continue for months to promote the idea in the public mind that Trump and his voters were racists, and therefore to augment the African American turnout enough to swing the close states to Biden. Trump won a larger percentage of the African American vote than in 2016, but the Democrats minimized the increase. Of course, it could also have been Biden's choice of Kamala Harris as his running mate that augmented African American turnout, so it is impossible to say for sure. However, I do not believe the rioting would have been permitted to continue for more than a couple days if Ms. Clinton had been elected president in 2016, as it would have been seen to undermine her authority as president. In that regard, my view is that the rioting was a political event, orchestrated by Democrats in government and media to undermine Trump.

I also believe that Covid would have been presented differently to the public if Ms. Clinton had been president. If the same events had happened in her administration, she would have been characterized as orchestrating a vigorous and successful response. In fact, the initial response to Trump's

13

efforts were positive, as the governors of New York and California, no political friends of Trump, admitted:

"This is not time to bicker," California Democratic Gov. Gavin Newsom said on CNN. "Let me just be candid with you. I'd be lying to you to say that [Trump] hasn't been responsive to our needs. He has. And so, as a sort of an offer of objectivity, I have to acknowledge that publicly. The fact is, every time that I've called the president, he's quickly gotten on the line. When we asked to get the support for that [USNS] Mercy ship in Southern California, he was able to direct that in real-time. We've got 2,000 of these field medical sites that are up, almost all operational now in the state, because of his support. Those are the facts."

New York's Governor Cuomo said Trump is "fully engaged on trying to help New York," and has been "very creative and energetic."

That was the true story, but during the campaign the Democrats sought to use Covid to obscure Trump's accomplishments in expanding employment, controlling the border, confronting China, and working with Congressional Republicans to improve the business climate. Cuomo's changed his story to:

https://www.theguardian.com/us-news/2020/oct/06/coronavirus-andrew-cuomo-donald-trump-pearl-harbor

Coronavirus: Andrew Cuomo blames Donald Trump for 'worst failure since Pearl Harbor'

October 6, 2020

In a new book, Andrew Cuomo blames Donald Trump for thousands of deaths in New York in the early stages of the coronavirus pandemic, decrying "federal negligence" he says led to "the greatest failure to detect an enemy attack since Pearl Harbor".

The unsolicited mail-out ballots instigated by Covid expanded the Democrats' ability to obtain votes, thereby cancelling Trump's advantage in expanding his base by eleven million votes. I believe the Democrats exaggerated the Covid crisis and harmed the public with excessive lockdowns to condition the public mind to believe that Trump had failed to stop the pandemic. I also believe the Democrats irresponsibly encouraged the rioting in the summer to foment the idea that America is a systemically racist country where racism and rioting could only be ended by voting Trump out of office.

Still, in the end, it was a referendum on Mr. Trump's performance as president. Trump's abrasive personality did not play well, especially in the first debate. He ran a poor campaign without Kellyanne Conway at the helm. In my view, his opponents in the media and in government bureaucracies whipped up a cacophony of misleading negative information about him and used misleading polls to suppress his vote. However, he constantly called them "enemies of the people." He had to expect them to pull out all the stops to turn the public against him. Blaming a failed campaign on a single cause is like the coach of a football team that loses every game blaming the field goal kicker. Maybe the kicker is not the best, but a lot of other things must be going wrong too, including the coaching.

On December 1, 2020 I discussed this with a blogger in an on-line business journal. The blogger wrote:

Character counts. Mr. Trump has made sheer nastiness a central driver of his election campaigns and often, of his presidency. His outrageous disrespect at the first debate with Biden -- a complete flouting of the rules -- was perhaps the single worst example of his nastiness. How does he then complain about rough treatment in the press?

Plus, Trump's behavior post-election has been typically narcissistic and an affront to America in the deepest sense (even allowing for his right to challenge election results responsibly where warranted by the facts).

For its part, the media's fault has been in falling for his provocations every time. Which they did, to be honest, because there were clicks to be had (that is, money to be made) in all those anti-Trump articles.

I responded:

That's the way I look at it as a Trump voter. Trump called the press "enemies of the people," so he knew they were going to go crazy attacking him. He certainly did his share of poking fun at his opponents, usually in funny ways, but sometimes demeaning. I think he lost primarily because he started to look smaller than

Biden, just as Ms. Clinton looked smaller than him the last time around. Not having Kellyanne Conway around for this campaign was way more debilitating than anything the press said about him.

Still, the press lied bodaciously about Trump, intentionally spreading bad information about what he said about Charlottesville in order to make him out to be a racist, and lying day and night about the Russian Collusion and Ukrainian Phone Call hoaxes. And then not saying a word about Biden, whose family was on the take from China, Ukraine, Kazakhstan, and Russia.

The press lies. But then it always has. As Calvin Coolidge said, "If you don't like it, don't read it."

My view is that our constitutional democracy has proved its worth once again in holding a rambunctious, continent-wide Republic together, as it has so many times in the past. Whereas before the election, city-busting rioting and even armed civil war was anticipated by many, the feeling after the election is that there will be peace during President Biden's administration, even if some (perhaps most) Trump voters believe the election was fraudulent. Even if it was, the Constitution is not fraudulent, and the verdict of the Electoral College, as determined by the state legislatures and the federal and state courts, must be accepted.

Is Trump Really Gone?

Is Trump, and all he represents, really gone? He has largely remade the Republican Party in his image, as a party that appeals to the working middle class, hard pressed to maintain their standard of living in a globalist era of porous borders and USA-made products replaced by imports.

Trump brought many like-minded Republicans into office. In Florida's 2018 election he helped defeat one of the four incumbent Democrat Senators who lost their seats. He assured the victory of Republican Ron DeSantis as Governor. In 2020 all ten Republican candidates for an open seat in my Florida congressional district vociferously pledged to support Trump. He won the state by three times his 2016 margin, helping to unseat two Democratic congresspersons, including the well-known Donna Shalala, in the process. Florida is loaded with up-and-coming Republicans aligned with Trump, including moderates like Marco Rubio. Other Senators like Lindsey Graham in South Carolina, Marsha Blackburn in Tennessee, and Senate Majority Leader Mitch McConnell of Kentucky have aligned with Trump. Lindsey Graham turned to Trump supporters for donations when it looked like his Democrat challenger would outspend him with over $100 million dollars. He said they came through for him, enabling him to convincingly win what had been thought to be a tossup race.

Will Trump come back in 2024 either running in his own right, or wielding a strong influence in choosing the nominee? I do not think he will run again. I think Republicans like Marco Rubio, Marsha Blackburn, Tom Cotton, Mike Pence, and Nikki Haley, who worked within the Republican Party and supported Trump as much as could reasonably be expected, will lead the party. Trump ended the dominance of the Old Guard of Mitt Romney, Paul Ryan, and John Kasich and cleared the way for the next generation. I expect the Republicans will nominate Marco Rubio in 2024.

If Trump's influence in remaking the Republican Party endures, and if Republicans take back the House and Senate in 2022, then elect their president in 2024, the Democrats' victory in 2020 will prove tenuous. Trump's election in 2016 might be seen as the beginning of a Populist Republican trend. If the Democrats gain momentum by winning in 2022 and 2024, then this election will be seen as the beginning of a trend toward Democratic dominance.

This may be one of those election cycles like 1860 where Abraham Lincoln was elected president with only 39% of the popular vote and probably would have lost if his Democratic opposition had not foolishly split the other 61% by dividing into three competing parties. Lincoln's Republicans were severely defeated in the Northern Congressional and state legislature elections of 1862. Lincoln feared he would lose the votes of his war-weary countrymen in 1864. The fortunes of war turned in his favor barely in time to enable him to prevail nationally, despite losing his own hometown of Springfield, Illinois, as he had lost it in 1860. Most people who knew him best did not vote for him. It wasn't until the congressional election of 1866 that Northern Republicans cemented their dominance and Lincoln's legacy became eternal.

Looking back on it, 1860 was the turning point of the evolution of the United States into a slavery-free Republic that set us on the eventual path of equal rights for all races. But it took a devastating Civil War and three more elections to confirm that decision.

Perhaps our election of 2020 will be seen in retrospect to have been the pivot point of the turn to our true political track for the future, the way the election of 1860 came to be seen after enough time had passed to view it in proper perspective. The predictive analysis I published in April 2019 may yet be our guide to recognizing the direction in which we will finally make the turn.

I will withhold judgment on Biden for at least a year because I have no idea how he will govern. I think his instincts are conservative, as Bill Clinton's were, but he is under tremendous pressure from the Left to radicalize the government. Jimmy Carter, another conservative Democrat, caved to that pressure and was undone by it. But, for the moment, I wish Biden well. Perhaps time will reveal that Trump has shifted the Republican Party into a more popular direction, as Barry

Goldwater did in '64. Goldwater did not prevail, but Ronald Reagan rode his coattails into the White House 16 years later.

Result vs. Predicted Outcome

How did the election result compare with my predictive analysis in April 2019? I forecast this election to be decisive in defining our political destiny for the next generation, or perhaps for the rest of the 21st Century:

If the Fourth Turning Theory of history is correct, then the post-WWII order that governed the world for 70 years was upended by the election of 2016. Where is the country headed now? Will Donald Trump become the progenitor of a new Populist Republican majority, or will he be replaced by Bernie Sanders or Elizabeth Warren on the Populist Left? Or, against all odds, will the Democrats be able to reconstitute their center under a leader like Joe Biden?

If the Fourth Turning theory is correct, then Donald Trump will either be the last of the Great Unravellers of the old post-WWII globalist order, or the progenitor of the new Populist / Nationalist 21st Century order.

My prediction for Republicans is that Trump will decide, perhaps reluctantly, to run again, and that he will prevail by the same electoral vote majority as in 2016. *I believe the Republicans will lose the Senate as voters reject their Establishment candidates. The election of 2020 will thus be a rerun of 2012 where a president who has accomplished 25% of what he promised, is nevertheless deemed worthy of re-election,*

23

even while the people reject his party's Establishment candidates in Congress.

I turned out to be correct about the Republicans losing the Senate, but wrong about Trump prevailing by the same narrow margin as in 2016, instead of losing by the margin of 45,000 in three of the states he won then. Here begins the Predictive analysis I published in April 2019. It may be useful to compare what I wrote then with how we know the election turned out:

Countdown 2020: A Predictive Analysis

This is a predictive analysis of the 2020 election, an election that may be decisive in defining our political destiny for the next generation, or perhaps even for the rest of the 21st Century.

If the Fourth Turning Theory of history is correct, then the post-WWII order that governed the world for 70 years ended with the election of 2016. Where is the country headed now? Will Donald Trump become the progenitor of a new Populist Republican majority, or will he be replaced by Bernie Sanders or Elizabeth Warren on the Populist Left? Or, against all odds, will the Democrats be able to reconstitute their center under a leader like Joe Biden?

Elections are usually written about after the results are in, giving them an aura of inevitability. We'll see how accurately we can anticipate the outcome of the 2020 election a year and a half before its outcome is known.

I've studied presidential elections going back to 1800 and have written about them in popular history magazines. In researching American history, I independently discovered the "Cycles of History" theory predicting that political realignments run in cycles, with another major realignment due around 2020. Although every day is a new day, and analogies to past events should not be overdrawn, I do believe that cycles of history have predictive value. As we will see, the unravelling of our political parties in the 2000's, and their realignment in the 2020's, has been anticipated.

I understand national politics. I've voted in Georgia, Ohio, Illinois, Alabama, Florida, Michigan, and Florida again. In most election cycles I travel the country from Key West to San Diego to Seattle to Michigan and back down the East Coast from New York to Florida. I don't talk politics obsessively, but I meet enough people to learn about the issues that concern them and can often anticipate how the majority will vote.

I predicted Barack Obama's electoral vote victory over Mitt Romney correctly in every state in 2012. In 2004 I predicted that Obama would be the Democratic Party's next presidential nominee in 2008. In 2013 I predicted that whichever party nominated a president like Trump would win the 2016 election. I voted as the electoral majority did, for Obama in 2012 and Trump in 2016.

I understand issues of globalization. I've founded an international business providing information systems to multinational companies. I understand the value of foreign trade, but I do not see it as panacea for growing our economy. I am married into an all-Hispanic family, so I understand how immigration adds value to the country. I've also experienced the illegal side of immigration and am ashamed of our business and political leaders who encourage it.

I'm not a political insider, but I've been close enough to politics for long enough to understand the propaganda both parties disseminate to make it appear that their interests are the same as the voters. While the interests of the parties and their constituencies often do coincide, there are times when the parties, funded by special interest donor money, work against the best interests of the people. We can make both parties stronger and more responsive by discerning the times when they are working for, and against, us. Then we can do a better job as voters of picking the people who are in tune with our interests.

My political views have been developed during decades of studying and writing about American History. They have been matured by debate in the electronics editions of leading business and economics journals, as well as during discussions of my book reviews.

Republicans, Democrats, and Independents who comment on my reviews of political books and blog topics mostly consider me a political analyst who gives all views a fair hearing:

- *This book and Alan Sewell's review are so insightful as to what needs to be done to save the economy and alas the country that for me several questions are begged.... Why don't we have a presidential candidate with the author's or Alan Sewell's comprehension of the economic problems?*

- *Alan, I agree and want to thank you, personally, as well. I thank you for your remarkable commentary supported by hard facts. You have changed my mind about some things through the excellence of your arguments, always supported by hard facts and documentation. You are an*

27

asset beyond compare to this community. Thank you so very much.

- *Mr. Sewell has made me rethink a number of ideas I thought were set in historical concrete.*
- *I only wish the country's "leaders" who fight endlessly in Congress to prevent the other side from making any progress would read this concise and well-reasoned review. It is better than reading a whole book about economics and succinctly states many ideas I have long held since I studied economics and then studied people. Excellent review and analysis that goes beyond the book.*
- *Great Review! I do so agree with every word in your review. I'll be reviewing, reading your books. Ever consider running for President?*
- *Alan, your comments restored my faith that our nation can become less divisive if people were able to listen with an open mind to a well-reasoned discussion of an important topic. On the other hand, I am very concerned that few people who share your leanings are as open as you are to listen to a reasonable discussion.*

I hope you will find this book tolerably fair in discussing the success and failures of both parties. I've voted for Republican and Democratic presidents, so I am willing to give both parties a fair hearing. I don't believe either party has a monopoly on wisdom, fairness, or integrity. I will explain what I believe will be the issues that drive the 2020 elections. I will try to predict each party's nominee, and the winner of the general election, based on my understanding of the voters' desired positions and the way I expect the candidates to address them.

The Center Dissolves

It's no secret that the center of American politics is dissolving. Establishment Centrists like the Bushes and Clintons --- along with dozens of formerly prominent senators, congressmen, and governors --- have been put out to pasture. More aggressively partisan candidates like Donald Trump on the Populist Right; and Bernie Sanders, Elizabeth Warren, Alexandria Ocasio-Cortez, and Kamala Harris on the Progressive Left have risen to take their places.

The unravelling began in the 1990's when thousands of family-owned and closely-held companies were acquired by multinational corporations owned and operated by Wall Street and international money funds. The small business ethic of looking out after the interests of customers, employees, and the community, as well as the profit-making interests of the owners, was discarded. Corporations owned by Wall Street only care about maximizing short-term profits in order to inflate stock prices and executive pay. Americans lost their jobs in tidal waves of {cost cutting, downsizing, outsourcing, offshoring, work force reductions, involuntary early retirements} and other euphemisms for dis-employing the wage-earning middle class and reallocating their paychecks, healthcare, and pensions to Wall Street money funds.

Economic inequality has increased. Employment security has decreased. Wages for the middle class are about the same now, inflation-adjusted, as 30 years ago. But healthcare and higher education have become prohibitively expensive. The economy weakened year by year until 2008 when the Great Recession slashed the country. The scars linger. A third of the country lost its livelihoods in industrial jobs that were removed from the country. Many people who lost their jobs, homes, and savings are headed into indigent old age. The economy has narrowed to the point where college degrees are necessary to quality people for jobs that don't pay enough to service the student loan debt. Offshoring of American jobs, combined with heavy legal and illegal immigration, maintains constant downward pressure on wages.

We are being buried under ever-increasing public and private debts. We are said to be growing our economy at 2% to 3%, but the national debt is also increasing at that rate. Since the national debt is now approximately equal to the economy, it might be said that no wealth has been created in the last twenty years, since every penny of increased wealth is balanced by a penny of debt.

Voters feel, consciously and unconsciously, that the Establishments of both parties have inflicted an economic catastrophe on the country that wounded the middle class. Tea Party Republicans, Progressive Democrats, and Populist Republicans have been unseating the Establishment incumbents in each party.

A dejected Democrat explained on election night 2016 why Trump had upended Centrist Hillary Clinton, who most expected would ride Bill Clinton's coattails into the White House:

https://www.dailykos.com/stories/2016/11/8/1593014/ -Election-night-2016-Finally-Liveblog-12

People are suffering financially in ways that we haven't seen since the 1920s…. The country is still poor. The job market still [expletive]. Bernie tapped into that anger and so did Trump. This was a referendum on poverty and what causes it.

People were seeking change in the elections of 2008 and 2016 and will be seeking it again in 2020. I believe that even President Obama, whose campaign theme was "change," diminished his legacy by becoming more of an old-time Establishment Centrist than the reformer many voters desired. He joined with Establishment Democrats and Republicans in bailing out corrupt banks with taxpayer dollars. This was not "change." Change would have been nationalizing the insolvent banks, zeroing out their stock, prosecuting their officers for financial fraud, and forgiving the mortgages of the failed banks' borrowers, whom the banks persuaded to borrow more money than was prudent.

But "change" was not to be had in meting out accountability to the oligarchy of "too big to fail" bankers! The only time Republicans and Democrats ever seem to agree is when their corporate donors ask to be bailed out with public

32

money. At those times they unite as a band of brothers. In 2009 they adopted Obama into their band of crony capitalists.

I'm a Republican who voted and campaigned for Obama in 2012. I rated him an "A-" president, higher than the "B+" he graded himself. I understand the pull of caution he felt as a relative newcomer, and our first African-American president. I believe he governed responsibly during an extraordinarily difficult time. He acted within the envelope of consensus that the Democrat and Republican Establishments supported. However, his surrounding himself with Wall Street Establishment crony capitalist toadies cost his party dearly.

The conservative Tea Party Movement not only massively defeated Obama's Democrats in the congressional elections of 2010 and 2014, but also retired many longtime Republican Establishment politicians. Obama was followed by Populist Republican Donald Trump, not by Centrist Democrat Hillary Clinton. Most voters wanted change, not the continuation of the Centrist Establishment status quo. When Obama didn't give them the change they wanted on the Left, they turned to Donald Trump on the Populist Right. A truckdriver friend, a lifelong Democrat, said in 2010: "Trump is the only Republican I'd ever consider voting for."

"Mr. Trump occupies an important place in the political spectrum," I wrote in a blog in November 2013, "that of being a Republican Populist. He understands that if we're ever going to get our economy back on its feet, the wage-earning middle class will have to prosper along with investors, who are recovering our fortunes in the stock market."

At that time, I didn't know Trump would be running for president in 2016. I thought the Republicans would nominate another out-of-touch ticket, like Romney-Ryan, that they nominated in 2012.

My feeling is that each party should nominate its strongest candidates. Competition of the strongest makes both parties more responsive to the people. In 2014 I didn't think Ms. Clinton could be elected, and since I'd just voted for Obama, I considered myself a Democrat. Vice President Biden's bipartisan work in the Senate became known to me, so I wrote him, suggesting that he run in 2016. Biden wasn't exactly a radical outsider. However, I felt that Ms. Clinton, besides being ethically challenged, was too much of an Establishment insider to be elected.

Many others were tired of Establishment candidates. I met a Liberal environmentalist in Vail, Colorado in summer 2016. He said he was going to vote Democrat but was favorably disposed toward Trump. "Trump is saying a lot of things that need to be said." I told him that I planned on voting for Trump but would not have been unhappy if Bernie Sanders had won the Democratic Primary.

Why were so many people so displeased with these Establishment Centrists like Romney, the Bushes, and Clintons, who they had supported before? Perhaps because centrist politicians, by definition, promote compromises that maintain the status quo that benefits the wealthy and well-connected. Many politicians are cronies of big business. When they retire from public office, they expect lucrative employment the companies they did favors for while in office. Thus, the bailouts of corrupt bankers under Obama's "change" administration was no different from what John McCain or Hillary Clinton would have done if they'd been elected. No matter which parties' establishment candidate was elected, the common folks were going to risk losing their homes, businesses, and jobs, while the corrupt bankers who wrecked our economy with financial frauds were going to be bailed out with taxpayer money.

Then there was Obama's "healthcare reform" that made the hospitals, pharma, and health insurance companies more profitable than ever, while their patients suffered grievously from extortionate overbilling. The Democrats took the input of the healthcare industry, wrapped government subsidies around it, and presented it as "reform." Although many people gained subsidized insurance, many lost their insurance when their health insurance companies tripled the premiums or withdrew coverage from markets where people couldn't afford to pay the premiums mandated by Obamacare.

President Obama likewise advocated the same dubious trade agreements as any Centrist Republican or Democratic Establishment President would have --- agreements like the Trans-Pacific Partnership, designed by multinational corporations to destroy American jobs and make us more dependent on imports.

The Establishments of both parties are paid by corporations and ideological think thanks to sign trade treaties that make it easy for corporations to replace American workers with foreigners earning far less. Our companies want to produce in Mexico or China, import into the United States, and sell at an inflated markup. They often launder the profits through overseas tax havens, without paying a fair share of taxes to the United States where the profits are earned. Corporations pay our politicians to keep the borders open to H1-B visas, unvetted "asylum seekers," and illegal immigration in order to pressure wages of American workers downward. They want to milk profits from the United States as if it were a giant cash register, without sharing any obligations of paying taxes, hiring Americans, and investing in the USA.

In prosperous times, people put up with this crony capitalist corruption. They were satisfied with Bill Clinton's and the Congressional Republicans' centrist governance during the New Millennium year of 2000.

We are fortunate to be alive at this moment in history. Never before has our nation enjoyed, at once, so much prosperity and social progress with so little internal crisis and so few external threats. My fellow Americans, we have crossed the bridge to the twenty-first century." - President Clinton.

We were soon to be plagued with massive internal crises and external threats. The Great Recession warned us that the old Establishment ways of making sham compromises, while ignoring the underlying problems that blocked the people's economic progress, would no longer be tolerated. It was time for real change, not for more Establishment sloganeering that masquerades as something new.

One of the Democrats' rising stars for 2020 --- South Bend, Indiana Mayor Pete Buttigieg just made that point:

https://www.cnn.com/2019/03/27/politics/pete-buttigieg-donald-trump-hillary-clinton/index.html

Pete Buttigieg just nailed what Hillary Clinton did wrong in 2016

Analysis by Chris Cillizza, CNN Editor-at-large

Updated 4:30 PM ET, Wed March 27, 2019

People didn't care as much about liking their candidate as they did about that candidate bringing about what they believed to be needed change. Four in 10 voters said that a candidate who could create change was the most important trait in their choosing of a candidate; Trump won more than 80% of those voters.

No surprise that Trump won. And it wasn't because of Russians.

The Fourth Turning

In the mid 1990's, "Generational Historians" William Strauss and Neil Howe employed forward-looking historical analysis to predict a "great unravelling" our economy and society in the early 2000's followed by a political realignment around 2020. They described these events in their predictive books **Generations** and **The Fourth Turning** published in 1993 and 1997.

Strauss and Howe follow the "Cycles of History" theory that anticipates existential crises occurring approximately every 80 years. I also believe this theory, having discovered it independently when I wrote my first book and magazine articles on American history in 1979-1987. Strauss and Howe identify the first three "turnings" in American history:

1780 – American Revolution

1860 – Civil War

1940 – Great Depression and WWII

In their books of 1993 and 1997 they predicted that the Fourth Turning would occur on or near the cycle of 1940 + 80 years = 2020.

They noted that every crisis is preceded by a period of unravelling. The unravelling of the 1940 crisis began with the global stock market crash of 1929. Fast forward 80 years, and we had a Great Recession in 2008 that began unravelling today's political establishments:

https://www.amazon.com/Generations-History-Americas-Future-1584/dp/0688119123/

https://www.amazon.com/Fourth-Turning-History-Americas-Rendezvous-ebook/dp/B001RKFU4I/

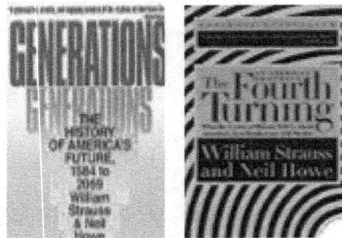

Events have generally panned out as Strauss and Howe anticipated. They wrote in *The Fourth Turning* in 1997:

The Fourth Turning is a Crisis, a decisive era of secular upheaval, when the values regime propels the replacement of the old civic order with a new one.

From this trough and from these dangers, the makings of a new social contract and new civic order will arise....

Soon after the catalyst, a national election will produce a sweeping political realignment, as one faction or coalition capitalizes on a new public demand for decisive action. Republicans, Democrats, or perhaps a new party will decisively win the long partisan tug-of-war, ending the era of split government that had lasted through four decades of Awakening and Unraveling.

Sometime around the year 2005, perhaps a few years before or after, America will enter the Fourth Turning... In retrospect, the spark might seem as ominous as a financial crash, as ordinary as a national election, or as trivial as a Tea Party.

The following circa-2005 scenarios might seem plausible: Beset by a fiscal crisis, a state lays claim to its residents' federal tax monies. Declaring this an act of secession, the president obtains a federal injunction. The governor refuses to back down. Federal marshals enforce the court order. Similar tax rebellions spring up in other states. Treasury bill auctions are suspended. Militia violence breaks out. Cyberterrorists destroy IRS databases. U.S. special forces are put on alert. Demands issue for a new Constitutional Convention.

A global terrorist group blows up an aircraft and announces it possesses portable nuclear weapons. The United States and its allies launch a preemptive strike.

...An impasse over the federal budget reaches a stalemate. The president and Congress both refuse to back down, triggering a near-total government shutdown. The president declares emergency powers. Congress rescinds his authority.

At home and abroad, these events will reflect the tearing of the civic fabric at points of extreme vulnerability...

...as the Crisis mood congeals, people will come to the jarring realization that they have grown helplessly dependent on a teetering edifice of anonymous transactions and paper guarantees. Many Americans won't know where their savings are,

41

who their employer is, what their pension is, or how their government works.

*This might result in a **Great Devaluation**, a severe drop in the market price of most financial and real assets.... As assets devalue, trust will further disintegrate, which will cause assets to devalue further, and so on....*

With savings worth less, the new elders will become more dependent on government, just as government becomes less able to pay benefits to them. With taxes hiked, the new mid-lifers will get to pocket even less of their peak-year incomes. With job offers dwindling, the new youth will face even taller barricades against their future.

Before long, America's old civic order will seem ruined beyond repair. People will feel like a magnet has passed over society's disk drive, blanking out the social contract, wiping out old deals, clearing the books of vast unpayable promises to which people had once felt entitled. The economy could reach a trough that may look to be the start of a depression. With American weaknesses newly exposed, foreign dangers could erupt.

If the Crisis catalyst comes on schedule, around the year 2005, then the climax will be due around 2020, the resolution around 2026.

Strauss, William. The Fourth Turning: What the Cycles of History Tell Us About America's Next Rendezvous with Destiny (p. 276-307). Crown/Archetype. Kindle Edition.

Dr. Robert Reich --- a moderately liberal economist, political commentator, and former Secretary of Labor --- also predicted an upheaval in the United States in 2020. He made this prediction in his book *Aftershock* published in 2013:

https://www.amazon.com/dp/0345807227/

The 2020 Election November 3, 2020.

The newly formed Independence Party pulls enough votes away from both the Republican and Democratic candidates to give its own candidate, Margaret Jones, a plurality of votes, an electoral college victory, and the presidency. A significant number of Independence Party members have also taken seats away from Democrats and Republicans in Congress.

The platform of the Independence Party, as well as its message, is clear and uncompromising: zero tolerance of illegal immigrants; a freeze on legal immigration from Latin America, Africa, and Asia; increased tariffs on all imports; a ban on American companies moving their operations to another country or outsourcing abroad; a prohibition on foreign "sovereign wealth funds" investing in the United States. America will withdraw from the United Nations, the World Trade Organization, the World Bank, and the International Monetary Fund; end all "involvements" in foreign countries; refuse to pay any more interest on our debt to China, essentially defaulting on it; and stop trading with China unless China freely floats its currency.

Profitable companies will be prohibited from laying off workers and cutting payrolls. The federal budget must always be balanced. The Federal Reserve will be abolished. Banks will be allowed only to take deposits and make loans. Investment banking will be prohibited. Anyone found to have engaged in insider trading, stock manipulation, or securities fraud will face imprisonment for no less than ten years.

Finally, but not least: In order for the government to balance the budget, provide for national defense, guard our borders, and pay down the national debt, all personal incomes will be capped at $500,000 per year; earnings in excess of that amount will be taxed at 100 percent. Incomes above $250,000 are to be taxed at 80 percent. The capital gains rate will be 80 percent. All net worth above $100,000 will be subject to a 2 percent annual wealth tax. Any American found to be sheltering his income in a foreign nation will be stripped of his U.S. citizenship.

In her victory speech, president-elect Jones is defiant: My fellow Americans: You have voted to reclaim America. Voted to take it back from big government, big business, and big finance. To take it back from the politicians who would rob us of our freedoms, from foreigners who rob us of our jobs, from the rich who have no loyalty to this nation, and from immigrants who live off our hard work. (Wild applause.) We are reclaiming America from the elites who have rigged the system to their benefit, from the money manipulators

George P. Bush, the Republican candidate, is irate. "I cannot stand before you and congratulate my opponent, who based her entire campaign on fear and resentment," he tells his supporters. Chelsea Clinton, the Democratic candidate, is indignant. "I would very much like to offer Margaret Jones my best wishes for the future. But I have to be honest: She and the Independence Party pose a grave danger to this nation."

The president of China appears before news cameras and says, simply, "The United States has committed a grave error." The presidents of the U.S. Chamber of Commerce and the Business Roundtable issue a joint statement warning that Margaret Jones and the Independence Party "will push America into another Great Depression." The CEOs of the four remaining giant Wall Street firms predict economic collapse... Mainstream pollsters, pundits, and political consultants fill the airwaves with expressions of shock and horror. Over and over again, they ask: How could this have happened?

Reich, Robert B. Aftershock: The Next Economy and America's Future (Kindle Locations 1118-1159). Knopf Doubleday Publishing Group. Kindle Edition.

That is almost exactly what happened on election night 2016, albeit four years earlier than Reich anticipated. Reich's hypothetical Margaret Jones combines Populist Right issues of trade and immigration with traditionally Progressive Left issues such as raising taxes on the wealthy to 80%. It would be difficult

45

to imagine this combination in a single American candidate. But it has happened that way in some European countries, notably Italy, where parliamentary governing coalitions of the Left and Right have combined to defeat centrist governments.

The question of whether the Populist Right or Progressive Left will prevail for the remainder of this century may be decided in 2020. It is possible that elements of both agendas will gain traction, but we are lacking the European parliamentary system of forming coalition governments based on a buffet of issues from each party. Our Constitution mandates a winner-take-all government. Our tradition is that during political realignments one party prevails and dominates the political agenda for one or more generations. If Trump prevails in 2020, the Populist Right will very likely cement its dominance. If the Progressive Left prevails, they will likely shift the country in their direction.

The 2020 election may thus be decisive either in strengthening and perpetuating the results of 2016, or in repudiating them and moving the country in the progressive direction. The only thing that is reasonably certain is that the old center will not return. The old controversies will be settled without compromise by the dominant side, which will have the power to impose its will without consulting the opposition much, if at all. The losing side will grumble mightily for a couple of years and then acquiesce to the new alignment. Our constitutional democracy will prevent the country from unravelling. The years of political division and rancor will be finished, and we will coalesce our politics around a new center.

Inequality and "Change"

The Great Recession was the catalyst for political change, as was the previous Great Depression that began in 1929 and lasted until World War II. Depressions are spawned by inequality --- when an excessive portion of wealth becomes concentrated in speculative assets owned by the well-to-do, and too little wealth is earned in wages paid to people of modest means. When people don't earn enough to buy the products their employers manufacture and distribute, businesses fail, and employees lose their jobs. When businesses and individuals can't service their debts, banks fail. The economy spirals downward.

That is what happened in 2008. We permitted, and celebrated, corporations taking away people's jobs in tidal waves of {downsizing, rightsizing, offshoring, outsourcing, re-engineering work force reductions, involuntary early retirements}. Then we wondered why they couldn't pay their mortgages and sustain the economy with purchases of consumable products.

The Great Recession ended years ago, and conditions have improved. However, the scars linger. Oren Cass explains in ***The Once and Future Worker: A vision of Renewal of Work in America:***

https://www.amazon.com/Once-Future-Worker-Renewal-America/dp/1641770147/

48

Yes, things looked better [in 2018] than in the depths of the recession, but they looked terrible as compared with the peaks of prior business cycles after long periods of economic expansion. Twenty percent of prime-age males were not working full time at the start of 2018.

This represented an enormous improvement from the 27 percent in that situation in early 2010, but prior to the Great Recession's start, it would have been the worst figure on record going back to 1986. In 2007, the figure was below 17 percent; in 2000, it was below 15 percent.

Median weekly earnings for full-time workers fell between the fourth quarters of 2016 and 2017, and median twelve-month wage growth (which compares individuals' earnings with their own income a year earlier) was lower in December 2017 and January 2018 than at any point in the prior two years and at any point from 1998 to 2008.

By 2016, the typical man with a high school degree did not earn enough for a family of four to clear the poverty threshold by even 40 percent.

Cass, Oren. The Once and Future Worker: A Vision for the Renewal of Work in America (pp. 23-25). Encounter Books. Kindle Edition.

There is a counter-argument that unemployment is nominally near record lows. Companies are said to have "millions of job openings that are going unfilled because we can't find qualified people to fill them." How can there be "inequality" if jobs are going begging, and people are moving up the career ladders as fast as they can climb them?

A lot of the "more jobs than applicants" propaganda is dubious. Many alleged openings are "jobs of last resort" such as debt collectors who harass people who are behind on their credit card payments. Or they're commission-only sales jobs for fly-by-night companies. Another source of "more jobs than applicants" propaganda is that any job, be it real or fake, gets posted dozens of times on the Internet. Many alleged "jobs waiting to be filled" are generated by "resume farmers" using internet postings as bait to lure people to send in resumes so that their personal information can be compiled into mailing lists and sold.

Companies are still refusing to rehire the engineers and managers they laid off in tidal waves of {downsizing, offshoring, outsourcing, work force reductions, re-engineering, involuntary early retirements} that led up to the Great Recession. We still have electrical engineers stocking shelves at big box stores; computer science Ph.D.'s sitting home in early retirement; and research physicists fired from their research projects and now programming arcade games for mobile phones. It is a tremendous waste of talent. Companies know where to find those people with experience if they want to hire them.

Instead they demand hundreds of thousands of H1-B visas for foreigners who'll work cheaper than Americans and who can be sent home if they become annoyed at working 24x7 or ask for a pay raise. Despite all the noise about how "robots and automation are doing all the work," the demand for illegal immigrant labor to do hands-on jobs that used to be done by Americans is incessant --- not because Americans won't work, but because people here illegally have no leverage to negotiate their off-the-books pay and are not protected by wage and hour laws. Companies continue liquidating thousands of jobs by mergers and acquisitions. They are still closing American factories and moving the jobs to Mexico and China.

Despite all the hype about how "people can make $150,000 if they learn to code," coding jobs are scarce and low-paying. For every "coding" job, there are about 17 applicants, and 15 of them are foreigners on H1-B visas. The jobs are often advertised as contract positions paying $35 to $50 per hour, with no health insurance, pensions 401K plans, or job security. IT jobs in much of the country pay about the same as they did 35 years ago when I worked them, when the cost of living was much lower. People come out of college with degrees that don't get them into jobs that pay enough to service their student loan debt.

Airline companies have also been relentless in beating down wages. Airline pilots, who spend around $250,000 and thousands of hours on training to qualify for a commercial pilot license, used to have high status and pay. Now it's become a low-wage job.

Airline pilots on regional airlines are paid $38 per hour, not much for such a such a responsible job, and only when they fly. Since they fly as little as one-third of the time they spend travelling to distant airports to connect with their plane and waiting for the plane to be readied to fly, their real hourly wage can be as low as $12.67. So now we have an "airline pilot shortage" because fewer people want to spend $250,000 on a job of high stress, high responsibly, and many days away from home, that only pays $12.67 per hour. Companies are pretending to believe that "Americans don't want to fly planes, so we have to bring in foreigners to do that job." We have just created an F-1 Visa to allow companies to bring in foreigners to be trained to fly American planes.

F-1 Visa

The F-1 Visa program is designed for professional pilot training, either airplane or helicopter, from zero hours to initial flight instructor rating.

*Once the Employment Authorization Document (EAD) has been received, the OPT period is 12 additional months, and **the student may apply for work as a commercial pilot in the United States.***

We are narrowing the jobs that pay middle class wages. When we can't get Americans to work for those low wages, we allow our companies import foreigners to work for less money, and the beatdown of American wages continues.

Employment is perhaps still less stable than it was before 2008. As recently as 2017, companies were still boasting about all the employees they were getting rid of:

The End of Employees

Updated Feb. 2, 2017 12:41 p.m. ET

Never before have American companies tried so hard to employ so few people. The outsourcing wave that moved apparel-making jobs to China and call-center operations to India is now just as likely to happen inside companies across the U.S. and in almost every industry.

...For workers, the changes often lead to lower pay and make it surprisingly hard to answer the simple question "Where do you work?" Some economists say the parallel workforce created by the rise of contracting is helping to fuel income inequality between people who do the same jobs.

Employers were saying then that they couldn't find qualified job applicants even while booting the employees they already had out the door. The ideal of the perfect employee is an unpaid "intern" who works for free. When employers say "we can't find qualified applicants" they mean that they can't fill jobs with candidates who already know everything and who will work for no pay.

There's no such thing as "a job that can't be filled." Employers can fill any job by raising wages to the competitive rate required for people to apply for that job. Employers have no more right to pay below-market wages than anybody else has a right to buy something for less than its fair market value. If labor were really in short supply, the efficient businesses would improve their business processes to the point where they could afford to pay higher wages to fill their open positions. The inefficient businesses that depend on cheap labor would close their doors, and their proprietors would go to work for the more efficient companies. As is the case of any other commodity, the demand for labor and its supply are always in balance.

There has also been a lot of noise about how people love to work "gig economy" jobs as independent contractors that pay low ages for intermittent work; or how people are thrilled about tearing up their cars as unlicensed taxi drivers. Those are jobs of last resort, not the major driving force for economic renewal that the gig economy propagandists tried to make them out to be:

https://www.wsj.com/articles/how-estimates-of-the-gig-economy-went-wrong-11546857000

How Estimates of the Gig Economy Went Wrong

Rise in nontraditional work arrangements was more modest than originally estimated, a new paper says

Jan. 7, 2019 5:30 a.m. ET

WASHINGTON—Two leading experts on the "gig economy" now say their estimates of its impact were too high, skewed by spotty data and the recession of a decade ago.

Alan Krueger of Princeton University and Lawrence Katz of Harvard sifted through new evidence to explain how, in a 2015

54

survey, they overestimated how people cobbling together a living from odd jobs, especially via apps like Uber, would upend traditional work arrangements.

And what about the notion that people removed from the labor force can find their way back to prosperity by retraining for "new economy" jobs that supposedly have an insatiable demand for employees? That is no panacea either. There are far too many people applying for the office "knowledge worker" jobs that we were told were the future of employment. Companies can hire surplus college grads for office jobs, so they are not going to take on the older unemployed. One study found that retraining for new jobs **reduces** laid-off employees' ability to find work, over what an untrained person can find:

https://www.amazon.com/Janesville-American-Story-Amy-Goldstein/dp/1501102265/

Laid-off workers who went back to school were less likely to have a job after they retrained than those who had not gone to school.

Retraining did not translate into greater success at finding a job. Among those who went back to school, the proportion who ended up with steady work was smaller than among the laid-off workers who did not. Worse still, more of those who retrained were not earning any money at all.

Goldstein, Amy. Janesville: An American Story. Simon & Schuster. Kindle Edition.

So why don't the unemployed move to boom towns like Austin or Seattle where the jobs are? Because those cities are crowded with job-seekers too. Wages are low relative to the cost of living. Few people with paid off houses in Ohio or Michigan are going to find any improvement in moving to Seattle and paying $2,000 a month rent for a small apartment in the far reaches of the metro area, while commuting hours into town to work a job that is not much above minimum wage. Living anywhere in the USA is perhaps harder than it used to be, even for young people in hotspots like Austin and Seattle:

http://highline.huffingtonpost.com/articles/en/poor-millennials/

Like everyone in my generation, I am finding it increasingly difficult not to be scared about the future and angry about the past.

I am 35 years old—the oldest millennial, the first millennial—and for a decade now, I've been waiting for adulthood to kick in. My rent consumes nearly half my income, I haven't had a steady job since Pluto was a planet and my savings are dwindling faster than the ice caps the baby boomers melted.

We've all heard the statistics. More millennials live with their parents than with roommates. We are delaying partner-marrying and house-buying and kid-having for longer than any previous generation...

This is what it feels like to be young now. Not only are we screwed, but we have to listen to lectures about our laziness and our participation trophies from the people who screwed us.

Like everyone in my generation, I am finding it increasingly difficult not to be scared about the future and angry about the past.

...Tyrone moved to Seattle six years ago, when he was 23, because he'd heard the minimum wage there was almost double what he made in Atlanta. He got a job at a grocery store and slept in a shelter while he saved. Since then, his income has gone up, but he's been pushed farther and farther from the city....

And it's already such a strain. Tyrone earns $17 an hour as a security guard at a building site, his highest wage ever. But he's a contractor (of course), so he doesn't get sick leave or health insurance. His rent is $1,100 a month.

We might dismiss this as the whiny lament of a spoiled generation that doesn't know how good it's got it. After all, my parents grew up in the Great Depression when people walked five miles into town each day looking for work. In my youth, before remote controls were invented, I had to get up off the couch and walk over to change the channel on the TV set! (as a comedian joked). So why are young people complaining about lack of opportunities?

Perhaps because they are coming out of college with mountains of student loans that they had to take out to obtain the college degrees that they were told would be their tickets to the middle class:

https://www.wsj.com/articles/the-job-advice-you-wish-you-knew-how-to-give-11557135000?mod=hp_lead_pos8

May 6, 2019 5:30 a.m. ET

Nearly 2 million students will emerge from U.S. colleges with bachelor's degrees this year. Many will enter a job market their parents barely recognize.

Competition for entry-level jobs is fierce, despite the tight labor market. Many applicants run a gantlet of internships and tryouts before getting a toehold on a permanent job. Career ladders of old have been replaced by zigzag job-to-job paths. Entry-level pay gains have fallen short of housing-cost increases in many regions, and grads' average debt has tripled since the early 1990s.

And that's if they can even get into a university. Lately we've been uncovering scandals whereby parents are bribing university staff with up to $500,000 to move their kids to the head of the admissions line; and where kids are told to pack their admissions applications with bogus information about activities that have nothing to do with education. Perhaps we've become a "who you know" society that depends too much on greasing elitist gatekeepers to get your foot into the institutions that credentialize your meal ticket.

Many retirees are also less well-off than they expected to be --- especially who were in their 50's and early 60's when the Great Recession hit. They lost their homes, savings, and businesses, and are entering a financially fragile retirement.

https://www.wsj.com/articles/a-generation-of-americans-is-entering-old-age-the-least-prepared-in-decades-1529676033

A Generation of Americans Is Entering Old Age the Least Prepared in Decades

Low incomes, paltry savings, high debt burdens, failed insurance—the U.S. is upending decades of progress in securing life's final chapter.

June 22, 2018

Americans are reaching retirement age in worse financial shape than the prior generation, for the first time since Harry Truman was president.

https://www.wsj.com/articles/bankruptcy-filings-surge-among-older-americans-1533641401

Bankruptcy Filings Surge Among Older Americans

Authors of recent study cite reductions to social safety net, shift from pensions to 401(k)s

Aug. 7, 2018 7:30 a.m. ET

The rate at which Americans age 65 and older are filing for bankruptcy has more than tripled since 1991 amid reductions in the social safety net and a shift away from pensions, according to a new study.

Older Americans are more likely than ever to find themselves in bankruptcy court, seeking protection from creditors," said the study written by academics at institutions including the University of Idaho and University of Illinois. It also said that among Americans in bankruptcy, the percentage of older people has never been higher.

Again, this might be considered over-emphasizing the negatives. People are having trouble stretching their retirement savings because they are living into their 80's and 90's instead of passing away in the 50's and 60's as many in previous generations did. It is wonderful that people are living longer. However, relatively fewer people can maintain continuous employment long enough to create a retirement nest egg. Layoffs in middle age force people to draw down their 401K plans, which they depend on instead of employer-paid pensions. The country is piling on debt to subsidize Social Security and Medicare because people aren't working as continuously as they used to, and therefore are paying fewer taxes into the system, while millions who work illegally aren't paying any taxes.

Perhaps people have good reason to feel less economically secure than their parents did during the great post-World War II prosperity of the late 1940's to the late 1990's. I grew up in the 1960's in a town of about 35,000 with a General Electric transformer plant, a chemical factory, and a textile mill. My father was a regional manager of a paint company. Our neighbors were factory workers. A young doctor lived around the corner. Everybody in that neighborhood could count on steady work at stable companies until they retired in their 60's. They could anticipate a future of steady employment and commit to buying houses and cars, and sending their kids to college, without fear that they were going to be unemployed in their 40's or 50's when family commitments are highest. Women could work if they wanted to, but many opted to stay home and take care of their children.

One income supported a family in those days, usually larger families than we have today. People with jobs in factories and offices retired with considerable wealth, never having had their careers busted by layoffs and early retirements. Today all those plants that provided steady employment when I grew up have been moved overseas. The people working them have lost their livelihoods, many in middle age, when it is hard to catch on somewhere else, especially when your industrial skills are no longer relevant in the USA.

Again, one can say that it is human nature to claim that "the old days are better than today" and to cherry-pick one's memory to make it seem that way. We remember the good things of the past and forget the negatives; while understating the improvements we have today.

However, we do expect unequivocal progress from one generation to the next. In most of our history we have had it.

61

Now many believe that they will live less affluent lives than their parents, and that their children will live less well than they. Student debt, middle-aged layoffs, and impoverished retirements are unwelcome developments. Considering the trillions of dollars of public and private debt required to prop up our economy, it seems questionable as to whether any real wealth has been created in decades.

Wealth that has been created is more narrowly concentrated among the highest incomes than previously. Corporation executives lavish themselves with more money in a year than most people make in their lifetimes. People in "protected" positions of government employment, including government-funded public education academia, are being paid well. People living in cities with rising real estate prices that can be funded with borrowed money are increasing their wealth --- at least until the next real estate bust puts them underwater. People who work for healthcare, an industry largely subsidized by government debt, are safe. People who work many other wage-earning, middle class jobs are arguably less well off and far less financially secure than were their grandparents in the '60s and their parents in the 80's.

Fair or not, that is the way many people feel, and the way many voted. If people thought the economy was giving them a fair shake at prosperity in the post-2008 world, then the status quo candidates of both parties would have prevailed in 2016. Instead they have been handed their hats and shown the door.

Destructive Inequality

In America, inequality is respected --- provided it is **earned** inequality. I've never heard anybody say that Bill Gates of Microsoft, Jeff Bezos of Amazon, Steve Jobs of Apple, or Sergei Brin of Google did not earn their great wealth. My family cried the day Steve Jobs died. "He was the best we had," said a TV financial personality.

Nor have I heard resentment against the self-made wealth of millions of small business people who take great risks, endure mind-breaking stress, and work endless hours to keep their businesses going. In small towns, the self-made wealthy often work the volunteer soup kitchens to feed the poor and make the donations to save the public libraries and keep the civics clubs going when nobody else will. The wealthy are beloved in America, because we all know that 3% of the people who have the talent and work ethic to do business pull the rest of us forward. Liberals and Progressives, who are often successful in business, are as protective of the rights of small business as any Libertarian.

We do not want a society where people are not rewarded for working and taking risks. Nor do we really want a society where there is zero risk of unemployment and financial distress. Sometimes the best thing that ever happens to people is when they get shaken loose from an old job and go on to something new and better. People must often become extremely unequal before they learn how to master life's challenges and reach their peak of excellence.

Let's call this kind of inequality that pulls people forward "constructive inequality." The owner of a business is celebrated for becoming a millionaire, not only as a reward for earned success, but because he or she elevates the employees who work for the company, and because all of them improve society by their work, and pay a portion of their profits and wages as taxes to keep their communities and the nation going. Constructive inequality a win-win, it's just that some people win more than others according to the value of goods and services they produce.

Inequality only bothers people when it becomes **destructive inequality,** the kind of inequality that is exclusionary and oppressive. It is a win-lose kind of inequality where some people win by taking away something that fairly belongs to somebody else. Discrimination against women, minorities, disabled, people over 40, and so on, are the types of inequality that aren't tolerated any more.

Other kinds of win-lose inequality are legal but controversial: for example, when Wall Street raiders buy a company for the purpose of stripping it of its assets. The raiders fire the employees and pilfer their paychecks. They load the company with debt and extract the working capital. After looting the company of its working capital, they either sell the company to an unwary buyer, or transfer any assets that still have value to a new company, then steer the old company into bankruptcy to void its pension obligations:

https://www.nbcnews.com/think/opinion/toys-r-us-bankruptcy-what-happens-when-wall-street-put-ncna876536

The Toys R Us bankruptcy is what happens when Wall Street puts profits before people

Vulture capitalists need to know that threatening America's working-class communities will be met with consequences.

May 25, 2018, 4:27 AM EDT / Updated May 25, 2018, 4:27 AM EDT

By Winnie Wong and Michael Kink

Ann Marie Reinhart Smith worked at Toys R Us for 29 years. Now, the Durham, North Carolina, grandmother is unemployed after being laid off as part of the iconic American toy store's bankruptcy and liquidation.

Smith is just one of more than 30,000 U.S. workers who face unemployment as the 70-year-old retail chain unwinds its business. The superstore's fall from grace is the result of a decade of disastrous management by the Wall Street firms that purchased the company and saddled it with billions of dollars of debt.

Meanwhile, the private equity barons who bought the company in 2005 have reaped hundreds of millions in extracted *profits, and top executives are leaving with $16 million in golden parachutes.*

Smith's story is a potent reminder of the human cost that Wall Street vulture capitalists inflict on working class people in their seemingly never-ending pursuit of profit.

It used to be that business owners and managers, who were paid the highest salaries, took on most business risk. If the business floundered because of their poor decisions, or because of circumstances beyond their control, they were expected to lose their jobs, or at least have their bonuses reduced.

These days the risk has been inverted and placed on the shoulders of the rank-and-file. Senior managers reward themselves with signing bonuses, stock options, and "golden parachutes" worth lifetimes of ordinary people's incomes, paid in full without risk, regardless of their performance. The rank-and-file will be the first to be let go if business hits a slow stretch. If business picks up again, the company will hire new people who work for less money, or they will move the business overseas where labor is cheap and import the product back into the United States.

Even in good times, companies often try to lay their people off in waves of {cost cutting, downsizing, offshoring, outsourcing, work force reductions, re-engineering, involuntary early retirements} to boost short-term profits so the bosses can earn larger bonuses. They want their money now, and do not care if they are debilitating the company by getting rid of the people who know the business.

Elitists are prone to saying: "That's how the market works. Companies are cash registers. You're only paid for what you're worth. If a company can find somebody cheaper overseas to replace you, then that's your fault. Go and learn something new."

These elitists who scoff at other people's unemployment are usually privileged people who have never had to scramble very hard in life or experience financial distress. The politicians and political consultants of both parties come primarily from this group. They are encouraging the rise of Socialists who respond:

"If business is nothing more than the the cash register of the rich, then we're going to make government the cash register for the middle class and poor. The country belongs to all the people. Every citizen has a right to adequate food, shelter, education, and work. If the elites won't play fair, we'll empower the government to enforce fair play by taxing the well-to-do and redistributing it to those in distress."

The Establishment Status Quo

The "Establishment" has been protested for most of my life. Back in the '60s, the old-time hippies lamented: "It's the Establishment, Man!" whenever they wanted to complain in vague terms about aspects of life that annoyed them. Conservatives in the 60's railed against "The Republican Establishment" that promoted patricians like Nelson Rockefeller for president and tried to keep renegades like Barry Goldwater and Ronald Reagan from leading the party. Today we hear that the "Establishment" is again opposed by Populists. So, who is this Establishment?

They're the people who run the big institutions --- the federal government, the big banks and corporations, academia, and most of the media. Their common interest is in organizing society with government at the top, and themselves at the top of government. Banks, big business, and academia are part of the Establishment because they depend largely on government funding and favorable regulation. Government in turn depends on them for financing of government debt and enrichment of politicians and government bureaucrats who want cushy private sector jobs after retiring with government pensions. The news and entertainment community are part of the Establishment because they are mainly staffed by liberal Utopianists who favor big government as the solution to everything.

There is nothing inherently wrong with any of this. The "Establishment" plays a leading role in all societies. After all, the people cannot know everything. They depend upon a governing elite who have the intelligence, knowledge, discipline, and experience to make many decisions on their behalf. People depend on large corporations, closely tied to government, to stiffen the backbone of the economy. Most of the time, the Establishment enacts policies that are the best that can be formulated given the circumstances.

However, there are times when the governing establishment becomes self-serving and out of touch. All social hierarchies are governed by people who would prefer that nobody oppose their views or question the legitimacy of the elites' privileged status. The Establishment of any society, be it a club, a business, or a government, will seek to suppress opposition that threatens its current leadership.

Americans got out from under the British Empire because the King's Establishment, was holding back the American Colonists' economic progress and taxing the people without allowing them representation in Britain's government. It wasn't long after our Independence that Americans of the Federalist Party Establishment tried to suppress the Populists of Thomas Jefferson's upstart Democratic-Republican Party, that both of our modern-day parties claim as their progenitor. Federalists passed the Alien and Sedition Acts:

69

SEC. 2. ...if any person shall write, print, utter or publish...any false, scandalous and malicious writing or writings against the government of the United States, or either house of the Congress of the United States, or the President of the United States, with intent to defame the said government, or either house of the said Congress, or the said President, or to bring them, or either of them, into contempt or disrepute; or to excite against them, or either or any of them, the hatred of the good people of the United States...shall be punished by a fine not exceeding two thousand dollars, and by imprisonment not exceeding two years.

Today's Establishment is still railing against "fake news" and "hate speech" with the intent of shutting down views that threaten the Establishment's agendas and status.

Establishments often become effete and corrupt. They are easily picked apart by external enemies. Adolph Hitler crushed the governing establishments of Europe's mainland democracies and would have remained master of Central Europe had he not attacked the colossal powers of the United States and Soviet Union. Today the Chinese are picking apart the United States by bribing our business and political establishments to ignore their aggressions. They steal our products, copy them, and sell them back to us. They swarm our businesses, government agencies, and personal accounts with cyberattacks. They require our companies that want to sell in China to produce in China. They refuse to buy anything that is made in the United States except in token amounts to reverse engineer and sell back to us and the rest of the world.

And what does our Establishment do in response? Nothing, except give away even more of our economy to China. Our big businesses only care about using China as a platform for cheap labor to make products at low cost, import them into the United States, and sell them at inflated markups. Our big businesses own our politicians. Thus, the interest of our Establishment is in selling access to the United States for their personal profit. "We can't upset China, because that will destroy our economy." Translation: "We can't restrict China's depredations against the American nation and people because we, the Business and Political Establishment, are in league with China to extract maximum wealth from the American people." The same goes for illegal immigration. Business profits by bringing illegal labor into the country, that is not covered by wage and hour laws, and that employers do not pay workers comp or taxes to employ.

The modern-day Establishment is not evil. It is just human, with all the positives and negatives of any collection of human beings. That includes being venal, self-serving, and conformist; and requiring its entrants to be credentialed with degrees, certificates, and employment by Establishment-sanctioned institutions

The Establishments of both parties loathe nonconformists like Donald Trump and Bernie Sanders, who spent most of their lives outside it, and do not share the Establishment view that a crony capitalist oligarchy of government, big business, and elite university and media people should decide the national agendas. The Republican Establishment was hostile to Ronald Reagan until he, like Donald Trump, won enough delegates in Republican primaries to go around them. The Democratic Establishment pulled out all the stops to derail Bernie Sanders in 2016.

The Democratic Party Establishment represents constituencies such as government employees, government-funded academics, environmental activists, "social justice warriors," and favor-seeking corporations. These people depend on government for their livelihoods. However, the top concern of the Democrat Establishment remains the protection of corporation profits, including subsidizing big businesses that operate in Democratic-controlled jurisdictions. It is no surprise that executives and major stockholders of large corporations donate generously to Democrats.

The Republican Establishment is also paid to represent the interests of big business, while ignoring the interests of the people as much as possible. We hear Republican Establishment candidates make statements that translate to: "We must cut Social Security and Medicare, because we won't have enough money to pay for those programs for the people, not after we get through reducing taxes on big business and the wealthy." They are paid to believe that tax cuts for corporations and wealthy investors are panaceas to spur economic growth, and that there is a perpetual labor shortage that can only be filled by opening the borders to foreigners who work for less money than Americans.

I may be critiquing the Republicans disproportionately because I know the Republican Establishment better than I know the Democrat Establishment. I know the Republican Party is loaded with political consultants who waste hundreds of millions of dollars running rigged polls and giving Republican candidates bad advice based on these bogus polls. A current Republican Establishment meme is: "Suburban women don't like Donald Trump's trade and immigration policies. Suburban women want open borders for more imports and illegal immigration." Another trick of the Republican Establishment is to tell candidates that people will be happy to lose their Social Security and Medicare so that big business and the wealthy can have another tax cut.

These fake polls ginned up by Establishment consultants usually cause the candidates they are working for to lose. Think George H.W. Bush in 1992, John McCain in 2008, Mitt Romney in 2012; and Jeb Bush in 2016, who washed out in the primaries after spending $100,000,000 to win three delegates. The most non-Establishment people in the Republican primaries in 2016 were Donald Trump, Ted Cruz, and Ben Carson. It is no coincidence that they were the most popular, and that Trump won the primaries and went on to beat the Democrats' Establishment candidate in the primaries.

You can usually tell which candidate is backed by the Republican Establishment by the stupidity of the campaign ads the Establishment consultants proliferate. They ran a vapid campaign for Jeb Bush in the 2016 primaries that practically invited people to vote for other candidates. The Republican Establishment's handiwork was very evident in torpedoing their preferred candidate for Florida's governor's election in 2018, thereby enabling the Trump-aligned candidate, who I supported, to easily prevail in the primaries. Party establishments played a large role in torpedoing the campaigns of John McCain, Mitt Romney, and Hillary Clinton. Successful politicians like Barack Obama and Donald Trump seem to ignore their parties' self-serving establishments, and campaign as themselves, instead of as cardboard cutouts of what their parties' establishments want them to be.

I no longer donate to the Republican Party Establishment. It is a waste of money to fund goofy political consultants who are working against my interests. I donate directly only to candidates I personally support. They all have websites, so you can donate to the people whose views you support and not worry about the party establishments sucking up the money and wasting it on bad candidates who represent the Establishment's interests, not ours.

I don't know the Democrats as well as I do the Republicans, but election results show the Democrat Establishment, to be, if anything, even more delusional than the Republican Establishment. Whenever you think the Republicans have shot themselves in the foot, you can usually count on the Democrats to out-stupid them by shooting off both feet!

Candidates on the Populist Right and the Progressive Left are reinvigorating both parties by removing the old Establishment fuddy-duddies and their self-dealing relations with their big money special interest donors. We're at one of those times when fewer people trust the party establishments than trust the Populist and Progressive party-crashers.

The Populist Revolt

The 2016 election pitted Donald Trump on the Populist Right vs. Hillary Clinton on the Establishment Center. The Progressives weren't in play in that election, at least not after Hillary Clinton defeated Bernie Sanders in the primaries. Thus, the election wasn't the contest between the Populist Right and the Progressive Left that many wanted. We'll likely have to wait until 2020 for that one. The 2016 election was a seen as a repudiation of both parties' Establishment Globalists by Donald Trump and Populist candidates aligned with him. Let's begin by asking, "Who are these "Populists?"

That question has been asked going back to the American Revolution when American Colonists, a considerable number of whom had Populist views, took up arms against Britain's King. Populists elected Andrew "Old Hickory" Jackson President in 1828, on Jackson's pledge to overthrow some elitist institutions like the Bank of the United States, while beating down early secession attempts to disrupt the Union. Jackson was perhaps closer in temperament and viewpoint to Donald Trump than any other president. Like Trump. He was a combination of factors --- wealthy, but with genuine affection for the common workingman and woman, and with patriotic reverence for the United States.

Populists rose again on the Great Plains in the late 1800s. In 1896 they combined with urban Progressives to oust the Democratic Party's Establishment and unite the Democrats under fiery Populist William Jennings Bryan's banner. Many Establishment Democrats found a temporary home in the Republican Party. It was an epic and energetic campaign of Populists + Progressives vs. Democrat + Republican Establishments, who rallied behind Republican William McKinley

McKinley won a surprisingly decisive victory for the Establishment in the 1896 election. He won it by convincing urban workingmen that he would prosper them by improving business and causing their wages to rise. McKinley's victory by courting urban workingmen was followed by Ronald Reagan in 1980 and Donald Trump in 2016. The difference is that McKinley was the leader of the Republican Establishment, while Reagan was outside of it, and Trump was antithetical to it.

Populists + Progressives lost the election of 1896, but they gave both parties a scare. Many of the reforms they fought for were adopted by the Democrats and Republicans during the following years. Our government today looks a lot like the Populists and Progressives of 1896 envisioned more than 120 years ago.

Now back to the question of "Who are these Populists?" They are a broad spectrum of people, but primarily from the middle classes of property owners, business owners, and employees. Their ambition to better themselves through business ownership and acquisition of property predisposes them to be

Conservatives rather than Progressives, who tend to be more aligned with the views of government, academia, and media.

Populists tend to be patriotic people of conservative family and religious values, although there are some flamboyant gays, atheists, and other people not of typically conservative social values leading the movement. Today's Populists count a fair share of blue-collar people who believe their jobs are being destroyed by excessive trade and immigration. Populists are most heavily concentrated outside of metropolitan areas, because that is where proprietor-owned farms, small businesses, and self-employed blue-collar contractors are most heavily concentrated.

Populists are subtly different from Libertarians. Libertarians generally do not like Populists, because Libertarians are ideological people who object to government in all but its most minimalist form.

"Give me liberty or give me death," said Libertarian Patrick Henry. But it was the Populists who started the shooting war. "The King says I can't farm my land west of the mountains? Who the hell is he to tell me what I can and can't do with my property?" When Populist property owners joined the Revolution, the fight was on.

"Here once the embattled farmers stood, and fired the shot heard round the world."

Populists, unlike Libertarians, are not ideologically opposed to government. They seek to overthrow the governing Establishment only when it becomes actively hostile towards them. 1776 and 2016 were two of those times. Another difference is that Libertarians are unconditional friends of business. According to them, business can do no wrong. "Free enterprise is based on the voluntary consent of buyers and sellers, and therefore is always beneficial." According to Libertarians, the banks failed in 2008 "because the government put a gun to their heads and made them lend money to people who were not creditworthy."

Populists, although firm believers in property rights, are a bit more skeptical of business, especially big business. Populists believe there are larger interests than those between the buyer and seller. Populists will resist allowing an unlicensed flea market to come into town and start peddling merchandise of dubious origin, even though there are people in town who are willing to buy merchandise on the cheap with no questions asked.

Populists respect the interests of the town's business owners --- who invest in the town, hire its people, and pay taxes to support the municipal government. Populists understand why it is necessary to call on government to keep itinerant flea market owners from setting up shop on Main Street to compete against them. Populists are likewise prone to banning imports from foreign countries that do not trade reciprocally with the United States or invest here and hire our people. They recognize that the bigger a corporation becomes, the less ethical it is inclined to be. The old-time Populists of the late 1800's railed against giant corporations:

The corporation has taken the place of the pirate; and finally, a bold and aggressive plutocracy has usurped the Government and is using it as a policeman to enforce its insolent decrees. The corporation has been placed above the individual and an armed body of cruel mercenaries permitted, in times of public peril, to discharge police duties which clearly be- long to the State. - James B. Weaver.

Wall Street owns the country! It is no longer a government of the people, by the people, and for the people, but a government of Wall Street, by Wall Street, and for Wall Street. The great common people of this country are slaves, and monopoly is the master. The West and the South are bound and prostrate before the manufacturing East. Our laws are the output of a system which clothes rascals in robes and honesty in rags. There are thirty men in the United States whose aggregate wealth is over one and one-half billion dollars. There are half a million looking for work. The people are at bay, let the bloodhounds of money who have dogged us thus far beware. - Mary Ellen Lease

Most of the time, Populists are "don't rock the boat" people. It is only when they believe their livelihoods are threatened by combinations of big government and big business that they become boisterous. There was a brief Populist fare-up in 1992 when the economy went soft and Pat Buchanan, Ross Perot, and Newt Gingrich rose to prominence in the Republican

Party. Prosperity returned in 1995, and the country did well under the joint administration of Centrist Democrat Bill Clinton in the White House and Newt Gingrich's Populist Republicans in the House. As soon as the Republican Establishment thought they didn't need Gingrich to maintain their majority, they tossed him overboard and ran the House as a Republican Establishment institution.

Populists did not rise again after the economy went bust in 2008. The fire started when Populists saw the Republican and Democrat Establishments join forces to bail out failed banks and big corporations, while the middle classes suffered grievous losses.

The conflagration became noticeable during the Tea Party movement of 2010 that cost the Democrats 63 House seats. It was all the more surprising following Obama's more than two-to-one electoral victory over John McCain in 2008. We heard then that the Republican Party was finished, that it was confined to a depressed inland territory of underpopulated states in the Appalachians and Great Plains, and that it would never again mount significant opposition to the Democrats. Populists were not yet out in full cry. They did not make their voice heard until it congealed all at once with the Tea Party Movement that returned the Republicans to their most dominant position since Reconstruction and rolled out the red carpet for Donald Trump to lead them back into the White House.

Many Republican Libertarians and Establishment Centrists were as flabbergasted by the advent of Donald Trump as were the Democrats he defeated. Republican Centrists are paid by big business that favors maximum imports and immigration. Libertarians have an ideological affection for free markets, which in their view entitles business to buy its products from anywhere it wants, and to employ anybody it wants, including people here illegally. It remains to be seen whether Establishment and Libertarian Republicans will reconcile themselves to their areas of common agreement with Trump --- cutting taxes on corporations and appointing Conservatives to the courts --- while being at odds with them over imposing government restraints on trade and immigration.

There is also some overlap between Populists on the Right and Progressives on the Left, especially in their mistrust of big business, and desire to improve the fortunes of the middle class. Trump voters and "Bernie Bros" often seem to get along better with each other than they do with their own party's centrist establishments. However, Progressives seem to be more interested in improving middle class fortunes by increasing the minimum wage and providing wider access to healthcare; whereas Populists are more interested in raising the pay of the middle class by restraining globalism, which promotes imports and immigration that enable corporations to beat Americans out of their jobs.

Globalization

The United States was founded on a globalist tradition. One of the reasons the American Colonists decided to get out from under the British Empire was because we wanted to trade with other countries on our own terms, without having the King impose tariffs on our imports and excise taxes on our exports to enrich the British royalty at our expense. American Colonists on the Atlantic Seaboard were a seafaring people, interested in trading with European nations. Even at that early date China, India, Japan, and other Asian countries beckoned as prizes of overseas trade.

We soon began looking to Asia's markets for our exports. In 1853 Senator William Seward, who later gained fame as President Lincoln's Secretary of State, said:

"Open up a highway from New York to San Francisco. Put your domain under cultivation and your ten thousand wheels of manufacture in motion. Multiply your ships and send them forth to the East (Japan, China, and India). The nation that draws the most materials and provisions from the earth, and fabricates the most, and sells the most of production and fabrics to foreign nations, must be, and will be, the great power of the earth."

As our economy shifted from farming to urban employment, our economic cycles of boom and bust intensified. The economy grew rapidly after the Civil War, but the growth was too erratic to maintain stable employment. The economy fell into a series of depressions with high unemployment and social disturbances that required the military occupation of major cities to prevent mobs of unemployed and starving workers from looting and burning them. In 1877 unemployed workers in St. Louis attempted to establish a proto-communist workers' commune that was defeated by the U.S. Army:

Walter Gresham, a Secretary of State during the severe depression of the 1890s, remarked:

"We cannot afford constant employment for our labor. Our mills and factories can supply the demand by running seven or eight months out of twelve. There is undoubtedly an element of danger in the present condition of society....I am not a pessimist, but what is transpiring in Pennsylvania, Ohio, Indiana, and Illinois, and in regions west of there may fairly be viewed as symptoms of revolution."

Our business and political leaders saw exports as the way to bail our domestic economy out of the crisis:

- *The increase of home consumption did not keep pace with the increase of forth-putting and facility of distribution offered by steam. Whether they will or no, Americans must now begin to look outward. The growing production of the country demands it. An increasing volume of public sentiment demands it.*
- *It behooves us to accept the commanding position the United States has among the powers of the*

earth. This country was once the pioneer and is now the millionaire. What is the present crying need of our commercial interests? It is more markets and larger markets for the consumption and products of the industry and inventive genius of the American people.

- *Future historians will call the events of 1898 the turning point of American history. The change was inevitable, had long been preparing, and could not have been long delayed. The American people had begun to realize that their industrial and commercial development should not be checked by the limitation of the demands of the home market, but must be furthered by free access to all markets; that to secure such access the nation must be formidable not merely in its wants and wishes and latent capabilities but in the means at hand wherewith to readily exert and enforce them.*

Our trading ambitions differed from those of the other Great Powers, which by the mid-1800s included Russia and Japan as well as the European empires. Those nations sought to impose monopolistic trading empires upon conquered peoples. We did not seek to acquire large land areas with captive populations and turn them into colonies. We developed the concept of the "Commercial Empire of Trade."

Our "Commercial Empire" was designed primarily to keep American factory workers busy making products for export to Asia and Latin America, so that they would not become idle tinder for riot and revolution against their employers and the government. In the 1880's and 1890s, naval visionary Captain Alfred T. Mahan persuaded our presidents and congresses to build an ocean-going navy to enforce our trading rights around the world.

Our great leap across the Pacific occurred when we went to war with Spain in 1898. The war was said to have been waged to liberate Cuba from Spain's oppressive colonialism. However, our first act of war was to send our newly built Asiatic Fleet across the Pacific, in the opposite direction of Cuba, to "liberate" Spain's Philippine Islands colony. We annexed Hawaii, formerly an independent nation, in 1898 as a way station to the Philippines, while the Philippines became our primary military base in the heart of Asia.

Our interest in maintaining trade with China led us to war with Japan in 1941, after Japan attempted a brutal conquest of China. Our trading relations with Great Britain likewise made war with expansionist Germany inevitable in the two world wars.

Emerging victorious in World War II, we made free trade a foundation of peace and prosperity for the post-war world. We granted free access to our markets to our allies and our defeated enemies alike. We made our dollar, alone of world currencies, convertible to gold, so that other countries could receive our gold in exchange for their exports we purchased. We established trade-promoting agreements and organizations such as the General Agreement on Tariffs and Trade (GATT), the World Trade Organization, and The World Bank.

The effects of international trade were beneficial, perhaps even beyond expectations. The demolished nations of Western Europe were quickly rebuilt. Communists, who had been a prominent minority in France, Germany, Italy, and Greece, were made irrelevant by the return of prosperity. Incipient Communists in burned-out Japan faded away. The United States and our allies eventually convinced the Soviet Union and China to adopt capitalism. The Soviet Union disbanded. China became so prosperous with state-sponsored capitalism, that it became an economic superpower, albeit by using the United States as a one-way market to sell to, without buying reciprocally from us. Although Russia and China remain authoritarian states, they are much less virulent than the communist governments that preceded them.

We thus entered the 21st Century with a justifiable faith in free trade as an engine of prosperity and democracy, for ourselves and other countries. We believe that free trade is a foreign policy as well as economic interest. We believe it decreases the propensity of foreign governments to attempt to increase their wealth by conquering other countries and looting them. We believe it destabilizes authoritarian regimes by bringing their people into contact with us and exposing them to our values of democracy and human rights. We believe it encourages all nations to join with us in a prosperous global trading community, as political allies, and friends with common values of human rights and democracy.

The other component of globalization is immigration. There is the feeling that we cannot be a great nation unless we are also a welcoming nation. In 1765 John Adams recognized that the destiny of the United States involves the destiny of Mankind:

I always consider the settlement of America with reverence and wonder, as the opening of a grand scene, and design in Providence, for the illumination of the ignorant and the emancipation of the slavish part of Mankind all over the earth.

We do not want to be like the stingy old man who has built a beautiful garden on his property and puts walls around it to keep the neighbors' kids from playing in it and maybe trampling on a flower. We want to shine forth to the world as the lamp of liberty and opportunity. We also believe that immigration brings new blood into the country. People in prosperous countries may become complacent security-seekers. We can become so affluent that we cease to take risks to grow our wealth in the way we did when we were lean and hungry immigrants looking to better ourselves.

Trade and immigration are our core principles, going back to the earliest days of our settlement. So, what went wrong with globalization?

What Went Wrong?

During the televised NAFTA Debate of 1993, Vice President Al Gore argued for NAFTA-WITH-MEXICO against skeptic Ross Perot. Vice President Gore promised:

http://ggallarotti.web.wesleyan.edu/govt155/goreperot.htm

"NAFTA will...greatly accelerate [our trade with Mexico]; we will have a larger trade surplus with Mexico than with any country in the entire world."

NAFTA was duly ratified by Congress in 1994 and signed into law by President Clinton. That turned out to be the *last* year that the USA ever ran a trade surplus with Mexico. The trade went into deficit in 1995, has remained in deficit every year since then, increasing to $81.5 billion in 2018:

https://www.census.gov/foreign-trade/balance/c2010.html

Mr. Gore promised that our "trade surplus with Mexico" would expand employment of American workers:

....We'll create more jobs with NAFTA....an additional 400,000 jobs [already], and we can create hundreds of thousands more if we continue this trend.

That promise was also turned upside down. My estimates, based on the transfer of automobile production from the United

90

States to Mexico following NAFTA, is that NAFTA-WITH-MEXICO cost us 440,000 lost jobs in the automotive sector alone. Anecdotal evidence backs that up. I once asked the owner of a manufacturing company in Michigan what was the worst thing that ever happened to him in business. Without a moment's hesitation, he answered: "NAFTA. Our work went to Mexico." I asked a distressed middle-aged lady the same question. "My job went to Mexico," she answered. The same happened after we signed GATT-WITH-CHINA, except that the job losses were in the millions.

These trade agreements substantially destroyed the industrial economy of the manufacturing belt that extends a thousand miles westward from the Delaware River in eastern Pennsylvania through the heartland of the United States to the Des Moines River in eastern Iowa. Progressive Democrat Michael Moore explained in August 2016 why the destruction of our industrial heartland would guarantee Trump's election:

https://michaelmoore.com/trumpwillwin/

5 Reasons Why Trump Will Win

Michael Moore

Midwest Math, or Welcome to Our Rust Belt Brexit.

Trump is going to focus much of his attention on the four blue states in the Rustbelt of the upper Great Lakes – Michigan, Ohio, Pennsylvania and Wisconsin. Four traditionally Democratic states....How can the race be this close...? Well maybe it's because he's said (correctly) that the Clintons' support of NAFTA helped to destroy the industrial states of the Upper Midwest. Trump is going to hammer Clinton on this and her support of TPP and other trade policies that have royally screwed the people of these four states.

And this is where the math comes in. In 2012, Mitt Romney lost by 64 electoral votes. Add up the electoral votes cast by Michigan, Ohio, Pennsylvania and Wisconsin. It's 64. All Trump needs to win.

Globalism halted our growth in manufacturing dead in its tracks and helped set us for the Great Recession of 2008. Our economy, and everyone else's, except maybe China's, remains weak, even to this day:

https://www.wsj.com/articles/markets-show-calm-after-brexit-delay-11553244944?mod=hp_lead_pos1

Stocks, Bond Yields Fall Amid Anxiety Over World Economy

By Akane Otani and Georgi Kantchev Updated March 22, 2019 *11:49 a.m. ET*

Global stocks and bond yields slid Friday as weak manufacturing data deepened investors' anxiety about the health of the world economy.

.... A report Friday showed factory output in the eurozone fell in March at the fastest pace in six years, while a gauge of U.S. manufacturing activity slipped to its lowest level in nearly two

years. The data sent bond yields tumbling, with yields on German 10-year debt trading in negative territory for the first time since October 2016 and yields on 10-year Treasurys at fresh lows for the year.

Meanwhile, stocks across the world retreated, with the S&P 500 losing 1.2% and benchmark indexes in France, the U.K. and Germany sliding more than 1% apiece.

"The global economy has clearly become an issue, with big headwinds there," said Tim Anderson, managing director at broker-dealer TJM Investments, pointing to mounting worries particularly in Europe and China.

The removal of our manufacturing economy overseas has gutted our industrial companies. General Electric used to be the most powerful company in the world. At its peak in the 1960's this one company accounted for fully 1% of GDP. Then it moved its manufacturing offshore and became a dodgy financial company. Look at it now:

https://www.wsj.com/articles/ge-credit-crunch-ripples-across-wall-street-1542220488?mod=hp_lead_pos2

Updated Nov. 14, 2018

GE Credit Crunch Ripples Across Wall Street

A steep fall in GE's bonds to junk levels is roiling credit markets, spreading pain and gain among investors and banks

By Matt Wirz Updated Nov. 14, 2018 4:10 p.m. ET Wall Street has a GE problem.

General Electric Co. GE -3.37% raised $115 billion of debt on a reputation as one of the U.S.'s safest borrowers. Now... GE stock has lost about half its value in 2018 and ratings firms in recent weeks cut its credit rating to BBB-plus, three notches above junk.

Globalization made it easy for companies to eliminate their American employees by moving their work to Mexico, China, and other low-wage countries. They now manufacture product with low-wage foreign labor, import it into the United States, sell it as an inflated price list, and pretend that the profits are made in overseas tax havens. The gains to the corporations' bottom lines were immediate, while the longer-term detrimental consequences of making Americans poorer did not show up until the Great Recession of 2008 and the Great Election of 2016.

As globalization took hold, an entire vocabulary of euphemisms for beating people out of their jobs entered the vocabulary: {downsizing, rightsizing, offshoring, outsourcing, re-engineering work force reductions, involuntary early retirements}. Corporation managements decided that employees were liabilities to be discarded in order to cut expenses, boost stock prices, and reward management, whose compensation became primarily based on stock price.

Globalization became the excuse corporation managements used to dis-employ their American workforces. "We had to let our American employees go, because they couldn't compete in a global economy." Globalists proliferate tidal waves of propaganda to make it look like their profiteering by removing Americans' jobs to other countries was an inevitable result of the same globalization that Globalists assured us would create jobs for Americans. Globalist talking points are riddled with contradictory inconsistencies. Here is an example from Ian Bremmer's excellent book *Us vs. Them: The Failure of Globalism:*

https://www.amazon.com/Us-vs-Them-Failure-Globalism/dp/0525533184/

Advances in automation and artificial intelligence are remaking the workplace for the benefit of efficiency, making the companies that use them more profitable, but workers who lose their jobs and can't be retrained for new ones won't share in the gains…..As a result, large numbers of U.S. factory jobs have been lost not to Chinese or Mexican factory workers but to robots. A 2015 study conducted by Ball State University found that ***automation and related factors, not trade, accounted for 88 percent of lost U.S. manufacturing jobs between 2006 and 2013.***

Then he writes:

Globalization creates new economic efficiency by moving production and supply chains to parts of the world where resources— raw materials and workers— are cheapest…. In the developed world, this process bolsters the purchasing power of everyday consumers by putting affordable products on store *shelves, but it also disrupts lives by killing livelihoods **as corporations gain access to workers in poorer countries who will work for lower wages.***

So, which is it? Are all these millions of jobs being lost because of automation not related to trade, or are they being lost because companies are firing their higher-paid American and European workers and moving the work to the cheapest labor countries? Of course, it is for both reasons --- that jobs are being lost both to automation **and** the removal of jobs to cheap-labor countries. However, Globalists misrepresent the proportions. They want us to believe that most jobs in manufacturing in the USA have been lost to automation. But then, in their unguarded moments of honesty, they admit that most jobs are being lost to "workers in poorer countries who will work for lower wages."

Globalists invent contradictions and obfuscations to mask realities they don't want people to understand. In this case the truth is that:

American companies move jobs out of the USA and into cheap-labor countries because they want to *avoid* spending money automating their USA factories and making their American workers more productive.

We are told that "free trade will create millions of well-paying jobs for American workers who will be busy making product that we export to other countries." Then, when American workers lose their jobs to imports from low-wage countries, we are told that "free trade is beneficial because it allows us to buy foreign stuff cheap."

We are told that "nobody works in manufacturing anymore because it has become a high-technology industry where all human labor has been replaced by robots and automation." Then we are told that "manufacturing is an obsolete primitive industry that should be moved overseas to more primitive countries where unskilled labor works cheap."

We are told that American workers are the most productive in the world and deserve the opportunity to prosper by creating product to export to the world. Then when the free trade treaties are signed, and American workers' jobs are removed to cheap-labor countries, we are told that it is because American workers are too lazy, stupid, mal-educated, and overpaid to deserve employment.

We are told that free trade is the keystone of prosperity. Then we sign "free trade" deals with many countries. Americans lose their jobs and the economy goes into a Great Recession and never recovers its pre-trade prosperity.

We are told that in order for our exports to be globally competitive, we must open our markets to unfettered imports from other countries that are purposed to destroy our domestic industries, thereby making it impossible for us to export anything.

We are told that foreign markets are pots of gold waiting to be exploited by U.S. companies, and that the USA is a stagnant market of declining business opportunity. Then we are told that the other countries are so fragile that they will all collapse if the USA restricts their access to our market to dump their surplus production.

We are told that we live in a high-tech economy where "robots and automation are doing all the drudge work" and that only people with college educations should expect to be employed. Then we are told that we must open the borders to millions of foreigners to fill all those jobs like scrubbing toilets, cleaning floors, and picking turnips --- jobs that pay very little and always seem to outnumber the high-tech jobs by at least ten to one.

We are told that manufacturing jobs will never return to the USA because they've all been automated. Then we are told that we can't bring manufacturing jobs back from Mexico and China because American labor costs (i.e. work done by human beings, not robots) will make the products unaffordable.

We are told that manufacturing means nothing to the USA because "nobody works in manufacturing anymore," but that it is essential for us to maintain NAFTA-WITH-MEXICO because it has allegedly "lifted Mexico from an economy dependent on oil exports to a manufacturing powerhouse with a rising middle class."

We are told that manufacturing of high-value products like computers, electronics, motor vehicles, aviation, and appliances should only be done in Third World countries that have cheap labor, but that the USA should import millions of foreigners to harvest our lowest-value, government-subsidized products like turnips, taters, beans, and "tree nuts" so we will have something cheap to export.

We are told that we can never bring manufacturing back to the USA because "Americans will never pay $900 for an iPhone." So, we import iPhones made in China, and we pay $900 for them.

We are told that high-value manufacturing jobs that pay $25 / hour must be removed overseas so they can be done for $2 / hour by Mexicans and Chinese. We're told that Mexicans and Central Americans must be imported into the USA to gather low value produce that is only grown in the USA because it is harvested by foreigners subsidized with indigent welfare support by American taxpayers.

We are told that manufacturing is a relic of the past that the USA should not be involved with any more. Then we are told that agriculture, which predates manufacturing by 10,000 years, is state of the art technology and the key to our prosperity in a global economy; so, we must open our borders to millions of illegal immigrants to come in here to hoe the land like their great, great, great, great, great grandparents did thousands of years ago.

We are told that we have become a "service economy" that will generate sustainable growth by relying on financial services, real estate inflation, and healthcare. Then the economy rolls over and dies when every large bank in the country becomes insolvent; stocks and real estate lose much of their value; and we are only able to purchase healthcare because the government is running up trillions of debt paying for Medicare, Medicaid, and subsidized health insurance premiums.

We are told that even if free trade is bad for Ohio and Michigan, that it is good for Mexico and China, and that we must care more about the well-being of foreign peoples than for our own American countrymen, who we are told are too lazy and stupid to be deserving of employment.

We are told that there is a shortage of skilled workers in the USA, and that is why American companies must locate their work overseas or bring in foreigners to do it here. Then we find that these are the same companies that laid off most of the skilled American workers they already had.

We are told that Americans are delusional in thinking we can build prosperity by running up an unpayable national debt. Then we are told that we need to import product from other countries in order to avoid paying taxes to our federal, state, and local governments that would limit the debt.

We are told that we must tax our people to spend $900 billion to defend our Asian "allies" from China and our European "allies" from Russia, but that we don't dare put tariffs on imports from China, Asia, or Europe to pay for our defense to protect these countries from each other.

And, we are told that we must fastidiously adhere to the "rules based international order" decided by supra-national authority, but that we must ignore national laws on immigration. According to Globalists, citizens of a country may be held accountable to international bodies, but illegal immigrants must be held accountable to no one.

Immigration has reached an all-time high in absolute numbers, and nearly an absolute high in terms of percentage of population. We have become an open borders country where anybody from anywhere can show up at the border, or sneak across it, demand asylum, and never show up for the hearing. People who are deported multiple times after committing felonies keep walking back in. Anybody can hire people here illegally and work them off the books without fear of prosecution. Any company can fire its American employees and replace them with cheap foreign labor under the false pretenses that "Americans don't know how to do these jobs."

People who favor open borders and illegal immigration are motivated by the following beliefs:

1. They believe social justice requires improving the lives of poor foreigners by letting them into the United States.

2. They are opposed to President Trump and are for illegal immigration because he's against it. They believe, correctly, that if Trump doesn't contain illegal immigration, his base will desert him, and he will fail of re-election in 2020.

3. They are business owners without ethics to comply with employment law. They want cheap labor without incurring expenses to hire it legally. This includes the Republican-leaning Chamber of Commerce and other big business interests.
4. They are politicians paid by big business to do its bidding, or a big-business media enterprise funded by big business advertising.
5. They want more liberal and Democratic voters.
6. They believe that the U.S. has a demographic shortfall and don't care who fills it.
7. They want the United States to look more like "the rest of the world" and therefore increase its racial diversity.

Liberal-leaning Democrats are inclined to favor illegal immigration for #1, #2, #5, and #7. They became especially interested in #5 when they lost the 2016 election, like the 2000 election, by a small number of votes in a few critical states. They want to tilt those states their way by repopulating those states with foreigners and training them to vote Democrat. Even if the Illegals don't vote immediately, they "vote" by being counted in the Census, and thereby inflating the Blue States' congressional representation and electoral college votes beyond what they are legally entitled to.

Republicans who cater to big business interests favor Illegals for reasons #3, #4 and #6.

Illegal immigration, and other asylum and H1-B immigration, often allowed under false pretenses, is troublesome. Any time the Establishment --- the politicians, big business, academic, and media --- decides that the laws of the country should be ignored, then the country is on the short road to anarchy and civil war. If the elites don't respect the law, why should the people? As Abraham Lincoln so wisely said:

"Let reverence for the laws, be breathed by every American mother, to the lisping babe, that prattles on her lap - let it be taught in schools, in seminaries, and in colleges; let it be written in spelling books, and in Almanacs; let it be preached from the pulpit, proclaimed in legislative halls, and enforced in courts of justice...let every man remember that to violate the law, is to trample on the blood of his father, and to tear the charter of his own, and his children's liberty."

Yet, advocacy for breaking the immigration laws are published daily in liberal and big business publications, such as **The Wall Street Journal:**

https://www.wsj.com/articles/one-more-immigration-try-1525993394

One More Immigration Try

*By **The Editorial Board** May 10, 2018 7:03 p.m. ET*

*House Judiciary Chairman Bob Goodlatte has introduced legislation to legalize Dreamers. But the bill is riddled with poison pills including **an e-Verify mandate** for employers, self-*

deportation of undocumented farm workers and stringent limits on family-based immigration. This would effectively force Republicans to choose between legalizing Dreamers and selling out employers.

https://www.wsj.com/articles/exporting-jobs-instead-of-food-1526600254

Exporting Jobs Instead of Food - The U.S. farm labor shortage is driving production overseas.

*By **The Editorial Board** May 17, 2018 7:37 p.m. ET*

.... immigration restrictionists are detached from the reality of the American farm economy and a worker shortage that's driving food production overseas.

*House Judiciary Chairman Bob Goodlatte is whipping votes for a bill that would limit farm worker visas to 410,000 annually, which would include the existing immigrant workforce. This isn't nearly enough. Worse, **falsely documented workers** [people here illegally who steal Americans' social security cards] would be required to come out of the shadows and return to their home countries before they can be readmitted.*

In these two articles we have the Editorial Board of the nation's most respected business publication calling e-Verify a "poison pill" and complaining that "falsely documented workers" who steal American citizens social security cards should be allowed to stay in the country without fear of prosecution.

104

Big business Republicans favor illegal immigration because they want cheap labor to beat Americans out of their jobs. "America is *our* cash register," the Republican Establishment and its big business donors are saying. "We're going to milk it for all its worth."

"If that's the case," say voters like me, "then let's see what the Progressives have to offer."

The Progressive Alternative

The Progressive Movement originated in the late 1800's as an alternative to the Commercial Empire theory of keeping American workers employed by selling our manufactured products to foreign markets. Progressives reasoned that the correct way to keep workers employed was to pay them wages sufficient to allow *them,* not foreigners in poverty-stricken overseas countries, to purchase the products their labor produced.

Although Adam Smith is revered in conservative circles as the father of laissez faire capitalism, he was also the father of the Progressive Movement:

No society can surely be flourishing and happy, of which the far greater part of the members are poor and miserable. It is but equity, besides, that they who feed, clothe, and lodge the whole body of the people, should have such a share of the produce of their own labour as to be themselves tolerably well fed, clothed, and lodged.

The progressive state is, in reality, the cheerful and the hearty state to all the different orders of the society; the stationary is dull; the declining melancholy. The liberal reward of labour, as it encourages the propagation, so it increases the industry of the common people.

The wages of labour are the encouragement of industry, which, like every other human quality, improves in proportion to the encouragement it receives. A plentiful subsistence increases the bodily strength of the labourer, and the comfortable hope of bettering his condition, and of ending his days, perhaps, in ease and plenty, animates him to exert that strength to the utmost.

Where wages are high, accordingly, we shall always find the workmen more active, diligent, and expeditious, than where they are low;

Smith, Adam (2013-09-12). The Wealth of Nations (Illustrated) (p. 30 and 31) Kindle Edition.

These questions of economic relations between employers and employees began to be discussed just before the Civil War. Abraham Lincoln described many facets of life with exquisite wisdom. He reminded us, before the Civil War engulfed his full attention, that we prosper when Labor and Capital (employees and business owners) work together in harmony:

Labor is prior to and independent of capital. Capital is only the fruit of labor and could never have existed if labor had not first existed. Labor is the superior of capital and deserves much the higher consideration. Capital has its rights, which are as worthy of protection as any other rights. Nor is it denied that there is, and probably always will be, a relation between labor and capital producing mutual benefits.

These questions deepened as our industrial development accelerated after the Civil War. Business began to dominate the

107

national and state governments and divert their interests away from the people's. Democratic President Grover Cleveland in his State of the Union Address in 1888 warned:

The gulf between employers and the employed is constantly widening, and classes are rapidly forming, one comprising the very rich and powerful, while in another are found the toiling poor.... the citizen is struggling far in the rear or is trampled to death beneath an iron heel.

Corporations, which should be carefully restrained creatures of the law and the servants of the people, are fast becoming the people's masters.

The existing situation stifles all patriotic love of country, and substitutes in its place selfish greed and grasping avarice.

Government, instead of being the embodiment of equality, is but an instrumentality through which especial and individual advantages are to be gained.

Communism is a hateful thing and a menace to peace and organized government; but the communism of combined wealth and capital, the outgrowth of overweening cupidity and selfishness, which insidiously undermines the justice and integrity of free institutions, is no less dangerous than the communism of oppressed poverty and toil, which, exasperated by injustice and discontent, attacks with wild disorder the citadel of rule.

Republican Senator John Sherman (brother of General William T. Sherman) warned his fellow Congressmen and Senators:

You must heed the [American people's] appeal or be ready for the Socialist, the Communist, the nihilist. Society is now disturbed by forces never felt before. Congress alone can deal with the [monopoly corporation] trusts, and if we are unwilling or unable there will soon be a trust for every production and a master to fix the price for every necessity of life.

Progressives of the late 1800's wanted to know why was there so much unemployment, poverty, and social unrest in the United States, at the time when economic progress had never been greater. Henry George asked this question in his widely-read **Progress and Poverty**:

THE NINETEENTH CENTURY saw an enormous increase in the ability to produce wealth. Steam and electricity, mechanization, specialization, and new business methods greatly increased the power of labor.

Who could have foreseen the steamship, the railroad, the tractor? Or factories weaving cloth faster than hundreds of weavers? Who could have heard the throb of engines more powerful than all the beasts of burden combined? Or envisioned the immense effort saved by improvements in transportation, communication, and commerce?

Surely, these new powers would elevate society from its foundations, lifting the poorest above worry for the material needs of life. Imagine these new machines relieving human toil, muscles of iron making the poorest worker's life a holiday, giving our nobler impulses room to grow. Given such bountiful material conditions, surely we could anticipate the golden age long dreamed of.

How could there be greed when everyone had enough? How could things that arise from poverty — crime, ignorance, brutality — exist when poverty had vanished? Such were the dreams born of this wonderful century of progress.

Yet we must now face facts we cannot mistake. All over the world, we hear complaints of industrial depression: labor condemned to involuntary idleness; capital going to waste; fear and hardship haunting workers. All this dull, deadening pain, this keen, maddening anguish, is summed up in the familiar phrase "hard times."

It is common to communities with widely differing circumstances, political institutions, financial systems, population densities, and social organization. There is economic distress under tyrannies, but also where power is in the hands of the people. Distress where protective tariffs hamper trade, but also where trade is nearly free. Distress in countries with paper money, and in countries with gold and silver currencies.

Beneath all this, we can infer a common cause. It is either what we call material progress, or something closely connected with it. What we call an industrial depression is merely an intensification of phenomena that always accompany material progress. They show themselves more clearly and more strongly as progress goes on.

Where do we find the deepest poverty, the hardest struggle for existence, the greatest enforced idleness? Why, wherever material progress is most advanced. That is to say, where population is densest, wealth greatest, and production and exchange most highly developed. In older countries, destitution is found amid the greatest abundance.

The great fact is, poverty, with all its ills, appears whenever progress reaches a certain stage. Poverty is, in some way, produced by progress itself.

Progress simply widens the gulf between rich and poor. It makes the struggle for existence more intense.

In the United States, it is obvious that squalor and misery increase as villages grow into cities. Poverty is most apparent in older and richer regions. If poverty is less deep in San Francisco than New York, is it not because it lags behind? Who can doubt that when it reaches the point where New York is now, there will also be ragged children in the streets?

So long as the increased wealth that progress brings goes to building great fortunes and increasing luxury, progress is not real. When the contrast between the haves and have-nots grows ever sharper, progress cannot be permanent. To educate people condemned to poverty only makes them restless. To base a state

111

with glaring social inequalities on political institutions where people are supposed to be equal is to stand a pyramid on its head. Eventually, it will fall.

*This relation of poverty to progress is the **great question** of our time. If we do not answer correctly, we will be destroyed.*

Progressives of the late 1880's began to understand that the economy was faltering because employees lacked the ability to consume what their labor produced. Businesspeople wanted to sell their surplus productions to the peoples of Latin America and Asia, but those were far poorer than Americans, and unlikely to buy much of anything we produced, a story as true today as it was then.

Progressives reasoned that we should be selling the productions right here in the United States. Raise workers' pay to the point where they could afford to buy that which their labor produced, and the factory owners would be able to sell everything they produced without having to rely on fickle foreign markets. Progressives understood that the economy, like a tree, can only grow in a healthy way if all its parts grow together in the correct proportions.

As a tree grows, its roots bring nutrients to the leaves, and the leaves shelter the roots from the sun. Together they produce the trunk, which binds the roots, branches, and leaves together. A tree that grows roots out of proportion to its leaves will falter because the leaves are not there to shelter the roots from the sun and prevent its heat from baking the water out of the ground. The leaves cannot be out of proportion with the roots, or they will not receive sufficient nutrients. The trunk cannot be out of proportion with either. If it is too small, it will not bear the weight of the tree. If it is too large, it will take the nutrients required for the leaves, and prevent their photosynthesis of the nutrients it requires to grow all its parts.

The different parts of the economy likewise must grow together to support each other. There must be enough profit from business to fund investments in new and expanded businesses, and to encourage business people to risk putting money in up front, that will be paid back over a period of years. Banks must be able to accumulate capital in order to lend it.

There must be enough jobs at sufficient wages to enable employees to purchase the goods and services that their labor produces. If a factory owner borrows money to expand factory production, the demand must be there to purchase the production and enable it to be sold at a profit. If it isn't, the factory owner will go bankrupt trying to service the debt. The factory will become worthless and the bank that loaned the money will fail. The factories will lay more people off and the economy will fall into a downward spiral.

The hallmark of a depression is a factory of tremendous productivity that is sitting idle because the people who work in it don't have the money to purchase what it produces.

113

Progressives believe the solution is to raise the workers' wages to the point where they can afford to purchase the economy's output. Consumption must be brought in balance with production and the factory owner will have the cash flow needed to serve the loans required to build the factory. Thus, the correct way to grow the economy is:

Production...Consumption...**production...cons umption...production...consumption**

The economy prospers when consumption and production grow together in lockstep, because consumption and production depend upon each other. Neither can sustain itself independently of the other. Conversely, the economy falters when production grows, and consumption doesn't keep pace:

Production...consumption...**production**...consum ption...**production**...consumption

Consumption failing to keep pace with production is the common denominator of economic depressions. Capitalists overbuild the economy beyond the ability of consumers to sustain it with their purchases. In the 1840's there was overbuilding of canals. In the 1880's and 1890's the overbuilding was in steel mills and railroads. In the 1920's it was overbuilding of factories to produce automobiles, radios, and consumer appliances. In the 2000's it was a tech bubble, made worse by the removal of our "brick and mortar" economy overseas. The next bubble will likely be the collapse of our healthcare system, which is being overbuilt beyond our ability to afford it

Financial and real estate fraud often accompanies these economic collapses. The wealthy pour their surplus capital into financial instruments and real estate, pushing the values far beyond what buyers can sustain. Then it all comes crashing down. The banks become scared and start calling in their loans, thereby choking off capital to business. The businesses get scared and start firing their employees. The employees get scared and stop making purchases. Farmers go bankrupt because unemployed city people can't afford to buy their produce. City people starve while farmers let their crops rot in the fields because it isn't worth the cost of transporting them to markets where people don't have money to buy them.

Progressives discerned that business needs a "flywheel" to store its momentum during boom times and release it during times when business is slack. Progressives reasoned that government should become the flywheel that evens out the instability of the private sector by:

- Putting the unemployed to work building highways, dams, and other public works projects during times when private employers don't have enough work to keep everyone busy.
- Printing paper currency to pay workers on government projects during the slow end of the business cycle to "reflate" the economy and retiring

the excess paper currency when the private sector gets back on its feet.

- Increasing the value of labor by imposing a minimum wage, a 40-hour week with time-and-a-half pay for excess hours; abolition of child labor; creating Social Security to induce the elderly to retire from work and allow the young to have their shot at employment.
- Imposing an income tax as a means of funding an increase in government spending and as a means of breaking up accumulations of idle capital.
- Empowering the government to regulate abusive trade practices of business, such as creating monopolies and price-fixing cartels; charging extortionate freight rates; paying under-the-table kickbacks to help preferred customers stifle their competition.
- Regulating banks to prevent them from squandering their depositors' money on reckless speculations.

Franklin Roosevelt later implemented these policies during his New Deal that sought to halt the economic rot of the Great Depression. He reminded us that capitalism has a social, as well as economic, responsibility:

My friends:

The issue of government has always been whether individual men and women will have to serve some system of government of economics, or whether a system of government and economics exists to serve individual men and women...

It was the middle of the 19th century that a new force was released, and a new dream created. The force was what is called the industrial revolution, the advance of steam and machinery and the rise of the forerunners of the modern industrial plant.

In retrospect we can now see that the turn of the tide came with the turn of the century. We were reaching our last frontier; there was no more free land and our industrial combinations had become great uncontrolled and irresponsible units of power within the state. The cry was raised against the great corporations.

A glance at the situation today only too clearly indicates that equality of opportunity as we have known it no longer exists...

Clearly, all these calls for a re-appraisal of values. The day of enlightened administration has come.

The Declaration of Independence discusses the problem of Government in terms of a contract. The terms of that contract are as old as the Republic, and as new as the new economic order.

Every man has a right to life; and this means that he has also a right to make a comfortable living. He may by sloth or crime decline to exercise that right; but it may

not be denied him. We have no actual famine or death; our industrial and agricultural mechanism can produce enough and to spare. Our government formal and informal, political and economic, owes to everyone an avenue to possess himself of a portion of that plenty sufficient for his needs, through his own work.

We must build toward the time when a major depression cannot occur again; and if this means sacrificing the easy profits of inflationist booms, then let them go; and good riddance. Faith in America, faith in our tradition of personal responsibility, faith in our institutions, faith in ourselves demands that we recognize the new terms of the old social contract.

We shall fulfill them, as we fulfilled the obligation of the apparent Utopia which Jefferson imagined for us in 1776. We must do so, lest a rising tide of misery engendered by our common failure, engulf us all. But failure is not an American habit; and in the strength of great hope we must all shoulder our common load.

Progressivism as well as Populism animates the American spirit. Both come to the forefront of politics when inequality derails the economy.

Issues for 2020

I believe the campaign for 2020 will be the contest between Republican Populists and Democrat Progressives that many wanted in 2016, when Bernie Sanders was seen by left-of-center people as the right challenger to Trump. I believe these issues will be campaigned on:

Capitalism or Socialism?

The 2020 campaign will be framed as a question of how to remediate income and wealth inequality in the fairest way that preserves capitalism while rendering it more socially responsible.

My view is that capitalism is the highest expression of economic freedom. It brings together the inventor, the marketer, the consumer, and the financier who together turn ideas into marketable goods and services that consumers want to buy. It creates positive feedback loops whereby all the participants in the creation of a product or service --- from business owners to managers to employees --- are incentivized to work together to provide maximum value to their customers, who are the ultimate bosses of all businesses.

The human mind operating in a capitalist economy is empowered to create infinite wealth from the common materials that nature provides. But capitalism should be valued at least as much for its spiritual dimension as for its creation of material wealth. It encourages people to achieve excellence in their life's ambitions as inventors, scientists, businesspeople, artists, doctors, public servants, and a thousand other callings.

Capitalism embodies the defining spirit of what makes us human beings --- the idea of progress. People desire to make progress in our lives by learning new skills and putting them to work to improve their capacity to add value to ourselves. We desire to leave a better world for our children. Capitalism is the catalyst of humanity's progress. Communism is the instrument of stagnation and tyranny, because it denies people the opportunity to direct the progress of their lives.

People who live in unfree economies suffer not only material poverty, but poverty of the spirit. How many people born with the talent to enrich the world materially or artistically have been stifled by the constraints of unfree economies? It is no coincidence that the world's great business and technology innovators fulfill their ambitions in free economies like ours. So do a disproportionate share of the greatest artists and intellectuals. The capitalist economy provides resources to those who wish to enrich Mankind artistically and intellectually as much it does those who develop desirable material goods and services.

Capitalism shines brightest in small businesses that personify their owners' dreams of achieving excellence in the creation of products and services that the public desires to purchase. The owner whose name is on the business backs it with his or her reputation. Many businesses are started because their founders achieved a level of expertise that makes them too valuable for any single company to employ. Their extraordinary expertise compels them to seek personal fulfillment by servicing many customers, spreading their expertise far and wide throughout the marketplace.

As the successful business grows, its owners hire employees to build an organization with a shared mission to prosper by increasing their customers' prosperity. The employees are incentivized to become more skilled in perfecting the products and services the business sells. Their economic value increases as they, under managements' direction, become more efficient in producing the goods and services that make their customers more efficient. The economy moves upward in a virtuous circle that increases the prosperity of all who invest and labor in it.

Nevertheless, capitalism must operate at a standard of reasonable safety. If a rash of fatal accidents should occur on a particular stretch of highway, the highway commission in the jurisdiction would be remiss if they did not seek to improve safety by lowering the speed limits, improving visibility, increasing the police presence, and perhaps installing traffic signals at intersections of connecting roads. The highway authorities are not against anybody's right to freely travel the highways. They are just doing their jobs to make sure that everyone who drives prudently arrives safely at their destinations.

Likewise, the "capitalist road" must have rules of the of the road, speed limits, signage, and a police presence. However, we must not go overboard in paralyzing our economy with big-government intervention that primarily serves the interests of government, and perhaps a few "crony capitalist" corporations that feed from the government. Highway traffic can be regulated to ensure a reasonable standard of safety without the police setting a speed trap behind every tree for no good reason other than to gin up cash to inflate the salaries of the mayor and city council. Let's not forget Grover Cleveland's words:

Corporations, which should be carefully restrained creatures of the law and the servants of the people, are fast becoming the people's masters.

I believe that capitalism must be regulated to serve the public's interests, as well as private interests. Large corporations that control the production and distribution of the necessities of life, as well as the employment livelihoods of so many people, must not be permitted to use their economic power either to destroy smaller businesses with unfair competitive practices, or to destabilize the economy with reckless practices that lead us into financial collapses and depressions. Nor must they be permitted to create gratuitous unemployment, such as firing employees with long years of experience and good standing in the company, just so the executives can have a one-time bonus by re-allocating the employees' paychecks, pensions, and healthcare and to themselves.

Companies that extract profits from the public bear a social responsibility to further the public's interest. That means paying taxes honestly, obeying the law scrupulously, and treating their employees, vendors, and customers ethically. We require an economy that is as stable as practically possible, and not another 2008 debacle where executives defraud the public with shady financial speculations, destroy the livelihoods of their employees, and then run to the government, hat-in-hand, begging for handouts from the taxpaying public.

Concentration of wealth *is* a natural tendency of capitalism. Big companies and banks buy out their smaller competitors with borrowed money, becoming monopolistic and corrupt "too big to fail" enterprises that go bust all at once and sink the economy. The natural tendency of competitive capitalism is therefore to decay into corrupt crony capitalist monopolies that maximize profits by raising prices while destroying employment and cutting wages. That happened in 1929 and again in 2008. Without government regulation it will happen again.

Capitalism must be regulated as a social, as well as an economic commodity. The larger a company is, the more of a social impact it has beyond the company. Small Mom-and-Pop businesses should be lightly regulated. Corporations employing thousands should be regulated with a view toward social responsibility. Jobs are a social as well as economic necessity. Without work, social pathologies such as crime, family breakdown, addition soar. The United States is a fantastically rich country. There should never be a time when any of our people don't have means to earn livelihoods to provide for themselves and their families.

Capitalism needs to work for everybody. There should be no more permitting Wall Street money funds to buy companies for the purpose of laying off the employees who worked decades building the company, so the Wall Street executives can pilfer their paychecks, healthcare, and pensions; loot the cash till; and then steer the company into bankruptcy. Our society is not obligated to permit excessively destructive effects of immoral, socially irresponsible capitalism. Franklin Roosevelt was right:

Every man has a right to life; and this means that he has also a right to make a comfortable living. He may by sloth or crime decline to exercise that right; but it may not be denied him.

Large corporation executives should not be permitted to deny their employees of good standing the right to employment, except in cases where layoffs are necessary to save the company as a going concern. In those extreme cases, the executives must be made to share the burden that their bad decisions have created.

We must also recognize that unregulated capitalism is not the optimal way to produce and deliver some goods and services. Unregulated capitalism does not work well for essential services like electricity and water that everyone must have in a civilized country. We can't permit power and water companies, or even cable TV companies, to jack prices of essential services beyond reason, so we regulate them as licensed public utilities. I believe this is also an appropriate model for healthcare, as I will explain in the *Healthcare* section that follows. I believe that healthcare must become a regulated public utility that is privately owned but regulated and price-controlled by a public services commission.

However, we must not go to the other extreme of advocating Socialism.

Socialism is based on the theory that the people of the country collectively own its land, natural resources, and essential public services including banking and industry. In practice this means that the government owns most of the economy. The problem, of course, is that government bureaucracies are poisonous when applied to business. Socialist countries mire themselves in poverty for the many, and unearned luxury for the few. In that regard, socialism is even worse than unfettered capitalism. Opportunities exist in socialist countries only for people who make their careers in government or who bribe government officials to bestow favors upon them. Socialism provides a middling standard of living for five percent of the people, while the remaining 95% are poverty-stricken.

Democrats and Republicans agree that "America is not a socialist country." We desire government regulation of private business, not government ownership of business. Capitalism is too ingrained in America's psyche to be replaced by socialism. Even many Liberals and Progressives are successful businesspeople. They are not going to permit the government to tell them how to run their business. On the other hand, there is plenty of room to improve capitalism, especially at the large corporation level. I will discuss these proposals in the *Corporate Responsibility* section.

I believe that capitalism can be preserved, and the necessary reforms made, either from the Progressive Left or the Populist Right. Which every side can strike the most correct balance between preserving capitalism, while sanding down its rough edges, will prevail.

Healthcare

Healthcare is a microcosm of all the issues we will be debating in 2020. It falls under the inequality umbrella because it poses the economic and moral question of whether the poor are entitled to receive the same quality of healthcare as the well-to-do.

The "talking point" positions by party are roughly:

Establishment Republican: "Nobody goes without adequate healthcare in the United States [we know that they do, but we don't want to be bothered hearing about it]."

Libertarian Republican: "You're only entitled to receive the healthcare you can pay for. Get the government out of the way and let the free market work."

Populist Republican: "We want the free market to work as much as possible, but there is room for the government to control excessive costs."

Establishment Democrat: "Healthcare should be provided by the private sector, but regulated by government, with government paying for the poor via Medicaid, Medicare, and subsidized 'Obamacare' health insurance."

Progressive Democrat: "Healthcare is a fundamental human right that must be guaranteed to every citizen. It is the government's obligation to ensure access to adequate healthcare for all. It should be free, or at least billed commensurately with each citizen's ability to pay. If the private sector won't provide equal access to healthcare for all, then the government should."

The Republican Establishment's role in the healthcare debate was to ignore the issue. They left the field to the Democrats, so of course the Democrats took the ball and ran with it. Can't blame the Democrats for going for the win when the other team doesn't show up to play.

However, the Democrats were too overbearing on their first attempt at healthcare reform. In 1993, First Lady Hillary Clinton tried to outlaw private healthcare, and bring all of healthcare under the umbrella of single-payer government ownership. "Hillarycare" was defeated by hostility from healthcare providers, insurance companies, and much of the public. It caused many voters to question the Clintons' judgment, and to vote the Republicans into control of the House in 1994 for the first time in nearly forty years.

When the Democrats returned in 2009, they tried a more moderate version of healthcare reform. This time, they accepted input from healthcare providers and insurance companies. They succeeded in winning the support of enough of them to enable the Affordable Care Act aka "Obamacare" to pass Congress on a strict party-line vote by all Democrats and no Republicans.

I supported "Obamacare" because I reasoned that the following groups already have access to affordable healthcare:

- Employees of large corporations and government who have employer-paid healthcare
- The elderly via Medicare
- The indigent via Medicaid
- Illegal immigrants who by law must be treated in American hospitals at no charge
- Prisoners, including murderers on death row

The people lacking access to affordable healthcare were the working poor, who earned too much to qualify for Medicaid, were not old enough to apply for Medicare; did not have employer-paid healthcare, and who earned too little to buy health insurance from their meager pay. These people received minimal healthcare, and were often bankrupted by the first hospital bill, since a short stay in a hospital may cost more than they earn in an entire year, or even in their entire working lives.

If we are providing government-subsidized healthcare to the indigent, to illegal immigrants, and to prisoners including murderers on death row, then of course we must provide government-subsidized healthcare to the working poor. Nor should we deny healthcare to people who are unemployed because a corporate raider bought their companies and took away their jobs and health insurance. The lives of people and their families whose jobs are destroyed by corporate raiders are at least as valuable as the lives of corporate raiders. Why should workers' families suffer for lack of healthcare, while corporate raiders lavish themselves and their families with the best healthcare money can buy?

Obamacare improved access to healthcare by providing a sliding schedule of government-subsidized health insurance based on income, and by partnering the federal government with states willing to expand Medicaid coverage to the working poor. Obamacare worked well for me and my family for the first five years. One of my children, working in a distant state, who did not have employer-paid health insurance, was able to obtain a surgery that relieved a painful orthopedic condition that might have crippled him. My wife's brothers, recent immigrants working for modest pay, received Obamacare coverage that possibly saved one of their lives. That brother was denied adequate treatment for a kidney infection prior to Obamacare.

Denial of treatment for the working poor isn't supposed to happen in the United States, but of course it did.

However, Obamacare has flaws that are beginning to unravel it. Its fundamental problems were revealed to me in early 2016 when my insurance company cancelled the policy covering my wife and me. Obamacare's mandates had forced them to cover us for every conceivable condition, including many we don't want or need, while removing the maximum lifetime payout limit of $1,000,000.

The bureaucrats who crafted Obamacare did not understand the insurance business sufficiently to know that mandating unlimited liability for the insurance companies, combined with guaranteed coverage for preconditions, would make health insurance premiums unaffordable for the middle class who buy it on our own. In March 2016 our nationally-known insurance company ceased writing policies for individuals.

Only two companies still sell Obamacare insurance to individuals in my home market in Florida. Their plans had the same out-of-pocket deductible of $13,000 as my withdrawn plan, with no coverage of "contracted services" like ambulances and anesthesiologists. I purchased new insurance from one of the largest insurance companies in the United States. The premiums for my wife and I increased from $7,200 to $19,200. Imagine getting seriously ill and having to pay $19,200 in premiums + $13,000 in out-of-pocket deductible + $4,000 in noncovered "contracted services." Not many people find value in "insurance" that costs their families $19,200 a year when they're well, and $36,200 when they're sick.

There aren't any price controls to prevent healthcare providers from billing at extortionate prices. For example, a pharma company manufactures rattlesnake antivenom and sells it in Mexico and Australia for $100 a shot. They bring the product into the United States and mark it up to $10,000. Since it takes 14 antivenom shots, they are billing Americans $140,000 for a treatment that costs $1,400 anywhere else in the world. (I know about this due to a neighbor's daughter being bitten by a rattlesnake and being billed $140,000).

Snakebites are rare, but still no healthcare provider should be able to mark a $1,400 product to $140,000. This would be an unfair trade practice in any other business. More commonly people get pregnant, they have premature babies, they have surgeries, and they suffer serious injuries that require emergency room treatment. The billing for these procedures is also extortionate, and beyond the ability of anybody other than the ultra-wealthy to afford to pay out of pocket.

An acquaintance owns a medical equipment manufacturing business. According to him, hospital administrators have started paying millions for a robotic device that allows physicians to work from an office outside the surgery room. He says the machine has a time-out that renders it dormant after ten uses unless the hospital pays hundreds of thousands for a replacement chip. He says this device has raised the cost of surgery by 4x and delivers inferior results compared to hands-on surgeries. He says hospital administrators buy the robotic device because it allows them to inflate their cost-plus markups.

So what if patients have to pay 4x for inferior outcomes? The hospital doesn't care. They will mark up the price 300% and send the bill to an insurance company, which also operates on a cost-plus basis and gets to raise its premiums whenever healthcare disbursements rise. If the patient is on Medicaid or Medicare, the government pays the cost and adds the tab to the national debt, whose interest we pay with our tax dollars.

Instead of constraining healthcare cost inflation, with its cost-plus mandate, Obamacare accelerated it. Your insurance company makes you jump through hoops of going to a general clinic, then a hospital, then a specialist, when you should be going directly to the specialist. You waste thousands of dollars obtaining a recommendation to see an orthopedic or cancer or gastrointestinal specialist, when you already know you have a broken bone, a cancer, or a stomach pain. The clinics and hospitals tell you than an MRI for a swollen arm will cost $168. They bill you for $2,800, then another $1,600 for "analysis" by the doctors. This misrepresentation would be considered fraud in any other business.

And then there is Big Pharma peddling pills at astronomical markups that purport to do everything from removing toenail fungus to thickening eyebrows, and with a hefty dose to remediate erectile dysfunction in between. Many of those pills have side-effects that make people sicker than they already were, and few are effective enough for people to afford out of pocket.

Without price controls, healthcare costs and insurance premiums will continue to rise beyond people's ability to afford them. Much of the increase will be masked, for as long as possible, by the government increasing the national debt to pay for Medicaid, Medicare, and Obamacare subsidies. But eventually our healthcare system will crash and burn as surely as the unsound financial economy crashed and burned in 2008.

My take is that healthcare *is* an essential public service, and should be regulated as such, like water, electricity, and cable TV. Our expenditures on healthcare are not only out of proportion to the results delivered but are getting beyond what our economy can afford to pay for.

What solution would I implement? First, we must get over the notion that healthcare is delivered efficiently by the free market. Healthcare, being a life-or-death necessity, is one of the services least suited to the free market. Patients don't know enough about medicine to shop around for value, the way they shop for consumer products. They are not going to trust their lives or lives of their loved ones to a quack doctor just because he/she has a lower rate than a skilled surgeon. They are not going to let their children die because they can't afford $140,000 to pay for a snakebite antivenom that should cost $1,400.

When people are severely injured, they are not going to ask the ambulance driver to take them to four or five hospitals to compare prices while they are bleeding to death. And if you have a medical emergency away from your home you don't know whether the nearest hospital emergency room is "in network" and will accept your insurance. It is beyond ludicrous to make people pay a king's ransom for "health insurance" that would be considered a scam product in any other line of business.

I believe Congress should pass legislation enacting a Federal Healthcare Commission that defines what medical services will be offered to the public, and what prices can be charged by any doctor, hospital, medical device manufacturer, or pharma companies.

A simple way to set prices would be to allow healthcare providers to charge the Medicare price the government allows, plus an additional mark up of 50% for non-Medicare patients.

That would enable healthcare providers to make a reasonable profit, while preventing them from extortionate over-billing. It would also simplify private insurance because the government would be the negotiator of maximum allowed prices.

For non-emergency procedures, patients must receive a quote for the services to be rendered and the price that will be charged, just like the estimates they receive for car repairs. The

Federal Healthcare Commission should be the arbiter of billing disputes.

Before the free market folks start objecting about how "price controls result in rationing," we need to remember that all essential public services are price controlled. Electricity, water, telephone service, and even cable TV are regulated and price-controlled by public service utilities. There is never any shortage of these services. The prices are set fairly, the providers profit fairly, employment in these companies is stable, and the customers receive the services that they require. Healthcare is an essential public service like water and electricity and should be regulated as such.

We should give healthcare providers something in return for submitting to federal price controls. That "something" would be relief from malpractice suits. The Federal Healthcare Commission should have its own medical experts to adjudicate malpractice cases, and award compensation for genuine malpractice with public money. This would prevent the plaintiff's attorneys from gumming up the healthcare works with frivolous lawsuits asking for preposterous settlements and would relieve the regular courts of medical cases that juries of laypersons are not qualified to rule on.

I would also allow doctors, clinics, or hospitals who want to open an entirely private practice that does not rely on any federal, state, or local reimbursements, to do business on an entirely private basis. The providers can charge whatever they want for their products and services, but their cash-paying patients should have no redress for alleged malpractice or bad pills in the courts. The courts are backlogged and do not need to be hearing medical malpractice disputes.

Thus, there would be a dual public and private system of healthcare, as there is for public and private universities. The public system would be price-controlled so people could afford it, while the private system would be anything-goes for people who don't care how much money they pay for healthcare. Private insurance companies could sell policies to cover both systems. Medicare for All would be an option for the public system.

The party establishments will not implement a public-private dual system because their politicians are owned by healthcare providers and health insurance companies; and, in the case of Democrats, by attorneys who make millions suing healthcare provides. It will be up to Populists and Progressives to light the fire under healthcare reform, and therefore force the major parties' establishments to either join them or get voted out of office.

Trade and Immigration

Imposing stricter controls on trade and immigration were the issues that elected Trump in 2016. Because Trump is for those issues, his opponents in the Republican and Democrat establishments become even more adamant that we should keep the borders open to unlimited immigration and trade. Here again, I know all the arguments and counter-arguments for trade and immigration. I've worked for and consulted for multinational companies, have run my own multinational company, and am married into a multinational family. I've studied and written about the history of trade and tariffs. I know all the buzzwords like {Smoot-Hawley, Adam Smith, David Riccardo, comparative advantage}. I will state my positions in summary form:

On trade, I believe that we became strong and prosperous by understanding that manufacturing was, and always will be, the core of a strong economy:

Hamilton's Report on Manufacturers, December 5, 1791

The expediency of encouraging manufactures in the United States...appears at this time to be pretty generally admitted.

The employment of machinery forms an item of great importance in the general mass of national industry...if it is the interest of the United States to open every possible avenue to emigration from abroad, it affords a weighty argument for the encouragement of manufactures...

There seems to be a moral certainty that the trade of a country which is both manufacturing and agricultural will be more lucrative and prosperous than that of a country which is, merely agricultural. . . .

Not only the wealth, but the independence and security of a country, appear to be materially connected with the prosperity of manufactures. Every nation, with a view to those great objects, ought to endeavor to possess within itself all the essentials of national supply.

Secretary of State Seward's words are as true today as they were in 1853 when he wrote them:

The nation that draws the most materials and provisions from the earth, and fabricates the most, and sells the most of production and fabrics to foreign nations, must be, and will be, the great power of the earth.

Manufacturing is more than about just making things. It is part of the human spirit to acquire the knowledge and skill to create products of value. It is the pride of making something tangible. When we removed manufacturing from our country, we broke the spirit of the people with industrial traditions. Globalists did not dare tell people the truth about the poverty and spiritual hardship they were plotting to inflict on us. They promised "trade surpluses and jobs." They delivered poverty of money and spirit. The two parties' establishments wrapped themselves around the Globalists who spoon-fed them campaign money and cushy jobs. Anyone who wants to glean my complete positions can read them in my other books on trade and tariffs:

https://www.amazon.com/ebook/dp/B07DN3NZFN/

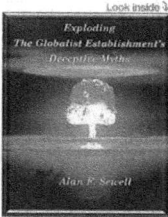

Exploding the Globalist Establishment's Deceptive Myths: On Trade, Immigration, and Politics Kindle Edition

by Alan Sewell ~ (Author)

Be the first to review this item

> See all 2 formats and editions

Kindle	Paperback
$0.00 kindleunlimited	$17.50
Read with Kindle Unlimited to also enjoy access to over 1 million more titles $6.95 to buy	6 Used from $16.70 4 New from $16.95

Globalists sold the public and our presidents and congresses on the theory that opening our borders to foreign trade would "create trade surpluses and millions of jobs for America's workers, who will be making high-value products to export." They told us that opening our borders to expanded immigration would reinvigorate our country with high quality people.

https://www.amazon.com/dp/B07HYYNV3G/

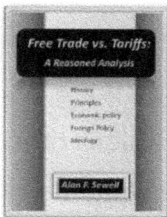

Free Trade vs. Tariffs: A reasoned Analysis Kindle Edition

by Alan Sewell ~ (Author)

Be the first to review this item

> See all formats and editions

Kindle
$0.00 kindleunlimited
Read with Kindle Unlimited to also enjoy access to over 1 million more titles $4.50 to buy

The debate over Free Trade vs. Tariffs is one of those issues that combines monetary and ideological interests and is therefore prone to inflaming opinions beyond reason. These issues affect people's bank accounts and their egos. People talk about them in shorthand phrases such as "Adam Smith, Milton Friedman, David Ricardo, Smoot-Hawley" as a way of saying, "I don't know enough about tariffs to argue the pros and cons intelligently, so I'll throw some buzzwords and 'appeals to authority' around and hope

https://www.amazon.com/ebook/dp/B07HLVJ3TD/

Why the Economy Died and Revived: 2008 - 2018: The Great Recession to the Trump Election Kindle Edition

by Alan Sewell ~ (Author)

Be the first to review this item

> See all formats and editions

Kindle
$0.00 kindleunlimited
Read with Kindle Unlimited to also enjoy access to over 1 million more titles $4.50 to buy

This is the 2018 Edition of the book I wrote during the economy's near-death experience of 2008. I was at the center of the crisis as a business owner and real estate investor. I saw it up close and personal in a way that most others have not. I want to present my view of why the crisis occurred in a short, readable book, and to reveal its most fundamental causes, which I believe have been intentionally obscured.

Follow the Author

I believe our trade should be managed according to the results that were promised:

"NAFTA will...greatly accelerate [our trade with Mexico]; we will have a larger trade surplus with Mexico than with any country in the entire world."

....We'll create more jobs with NAFTA....an additional 400,000 jobs [already], and we can create hundreds of thousands more if we continue this trend.

It's not right to promise that trade will create trade surpluses and jobs for Americans, and then say it's a good thing to run a trillion-dollar trade deficit and ship millions of American jobs overseas. It is not a good idea to pretend that chronic trade deficits are good for us when the government of every other countries believes that inflicting perennial trade deficits on us is good for them. It is not a favorable exchange to sell off our companies, our industrial knowledge, and our assets, and encumber our children with debt, to pay for imports of cheaply made gewgaws that are going to be in the junkpile next year. It is not a good idea to depend on everything from China, including most of our seafood, pet food construction materials, cemetery monuments, and everything in between.

I want our trade to be balanced, so that we are not running chronic perennial deficits with any country. I would balance the trade by implementing a Border Adjustment VAT (BAVAT) along the lines proposed by former House Ways and Means Chairman Kevin Brady. His proposal is a BAVAT that

140

taxes products sold in the United States at the rate of 20% *
(USA revenues – USA cost inputs). If your cost inputs come from
the USA, you get to deduct those before paying the tax. If your
cost inputs come from outside the United States via imports, you
pay the full 20%. If you produce product in the United States and
export it, you will receive a tax rebate of 20% of your USA costs.

We could tweak Congressman Kevin Brady's BAVAT by
treating products from our very few fair-trading partners like
Canada as if the product was made in the United States. Thus,
products sourced from Canada and a few other countries would
be taxed at the same low rates as our own companies are.

If the 20% BAVAT doesn't balance the trade with some
countries, then keep upping it with those countries until it does.
It might take a 50% BAVAT to balance trade with Japan and the
European Union, and 300% to balance the trade with China. If
they want the rates lowered, they can buy more from us, and
then we can reduce the BAVAT as the trade swings into balance.

Again, I have heard all the arguments against BAVAT
taxes. I have carefully considered the arguments and rejected
them. The United States is being bankrupted by trade deficits,
which by reducing employment and business investment in the
United States, also reduce our economic growth. Slower economic
growth expands our federal debt due to less tax revenue being
collected from a sputtering, recession-prone economy. We are
losing our jobs, our wealth, and our knowledge of how to
manufacture. These losses are cumulative. A point will be

reached at which they become irreversible, and we slide into poverty and probably domination by China and other countries that manage their economies for the best interests of their countries better than we manage trade for the best interests of the United States.

As to immigration, I want illegal immigration blocked at the border with an immense physical barrier, and the fraudulent "asylum" immigration and H1-B visas curtailed. We have a legal quota of 675,000 immigrants a year. That is enough to add a metro area the size of Philadelphia, Dallas, Chicago, or Miami to the United States every decade. That is enough. There can be 300,000 allowed for family unification, 300,000 allowed for merit and skills, and 75,000 let in as "asylum refugees."

I am married into a legal immigrant Hispanic family, some waiting 12 years in queue to obtain an immigration visa, being rejected twice before being allowed in. It is ludicrous to let people hop across the border without vetting. As to H1-B visas, companies should pay at least $100,000 per year per applicant for the privilege of replacing an American with a foreign worker. If the H1-B people are worth $100,000 a year, then bring them in. If they're not, then hire an American.

I believe that immigration is beneficial, and should continue with the 675,000 quota, but that it has been over-rated as a panacea that will somehow magically resolve all our chronic, self-inflicted problems. As immigrant author George J. Borjas writes in *We Wanted Workers*:

After all is said and done, immigration turns out to be just another government redistribution program. And this lesson sheds a lot of light on which groups are on which side of the immigration wars.... Immigrant participation in the workforce redistributes wealth from those who compete with immigrants to those who use immigrants.... Which side are YOU rooting for?

Illegal labor is not necessary. It is merely a convenience that enables shady business owners to profit by offloading their labor costs to the public. When Illegals are sick or injured, the public is taxed to pay their hospital bills. When they become too infirm to work, citizens are taxed to pay for their indigent old age. They put honest companies who employ legally at a disadvantage. Illegal labor slows down the economic progress of the country by substituting cheap labor for productivity-enhancing equipment.

Illegal immigration becomes even worse when it is done for fraudulent reasons, such as to repopulate the country in order to change its demographics and politics.

Above all else, illegal immigration subverts democracy and respect for the law. If it is OK to hire illegally, and thereby cheat honest employers by underselling them with illegal labor costs, then why isn't it legal to burn down your competitors' places of business?

Minimum Wage and Universal Basic Income

On the minimum wage and Universal Basic Income (UBI), I align with the Progressive view that the minimum wage is necessary and should be raised; and that the UBI may, if properly implemented, be an improvement on our current hodgepodge of social welfare programs.

The minimum wage is necessary to make sure that employees are paid for their work. Without it, unscrupulous employers would tell their people at the end of the week: "Your work is no good. I'm not paying you anything." The minimum wage also protects honest employers from being undercut by those who cheat their workers.

Here again, I know all the employer and Libertarian arguments for why there shouldn't be a minimum wage. Employers and Libertarians say that the free market should be allowed to set wage rates without a minimum wage. They also simultaneously claim that the free market **doesn't** work for labor and that we must open our borders to cheap foreign labor, including illegal labor, because they pretend to believe there aren't enough Americans willing to work for the below-market wages employers want to pay.

Employers and libertarian "economists" claim that eliminating the minimum wage would increase employment for the poor. This is unlikely for these reasons:

1. Employers never hire more people than they need. If the minimum wage were reduced from $9.00 to $1.00, they would not hire nine times more people. They wouldn't hire on a single person more than they need to do the work.

2. Cutting wages reduces the employees' purchasing power and thereby harms business owners. What kind of business owner wants a store full of poverty-stricken people wandering the aisles who are likely to steal something because they can't afford to buy the merchandise? Business profits more when employees are paid well.

Employers would love to have their employees working as unpaid interns, while the employers buy out their competitors and charge monopoly prices to consumers. Business owners don't care about free markets; only about profits.

Cheapskate employers shouldn't be able to hire people for a pittance while employers who pay a fair wage must pay taxes to subsidize the food, clothing, housing, and housing of employees who work at down-at-heels competitors. All employers should pay the same minimum wage in order to prevent a "race to the bottom" that ends with poverty and oppression, followed by riot, revolution, and the end of capitalism.

I also don't buy the "productivity myth" that postulates that increases in productivity lead to higher wages, so employees should stop complaining about low pay and wait around until their productivity improves. Employers never purchase productivity-enhancing machinery for the purpose of raising wages. If they buy a machine that makes 100 of 200 employees redundant, they are going to fire 100 employees, then cut the wages of the remaining 100, as there will now be twice as many workers competing for fewer jobs. Companies only spend money on productivity-enhancing equipment when the cost of labor increases. Raise the minimum wage, and then companies will start working on improving their business processes in order to make their employees more productive.

I would raise the minimum wage to $15.00 / hour for fulltime labor over 30 hours a week; to $20.00 for part-time hours under 30; and to $25.00 for "independent contractors" who pay their own taxes and have no rights of employees; and I would outlaw the practice of hiring unpaid interns. I would pass a law providing any "independent contractor" who is performing the role of an employee the right to be hired by the company as an employee after working 1,000 hours for hourly pay on the company's premises while using company tools and company supervision.

I would also give employers a break on one of their biggest annoyances, which is paying unemployment insurance of hundreds of dollars a year when they hire somebody. Employers should never be taxed for hiring people. Eliminate the burdensome and counter-productive unemployment taxes. If we're going to require employers to pay a minimum wage, let's not burden them with paying for their employees' unemployment insurance.

And that brings us to the Universal Basic Income, or UBI. A properly conceived UBI would eliminate unemployment insurance, food stamps, housing vouchers, and a myriad of other social welfare programs. It would also eliminate much of the social welfare bureaucracy that administers the programs. The UBI appeals to some Conservatives like Milton Friedman and Charles Murray. They like it because it gets the government's welfare bureaucracy out of the way and gives the recipients freedom to spend the money any way they want or bank it for a "rainy day" of unemployment or going back to school. I would implement the UBI according to the following principles:

- It is a total replacement for unemployment insurance, food stamps, housing vouchers, college tuition loans, and every other form of welfare.
- It is paid to every adult over the age of 18, whether they work or not. Those who work can bank it for a rainy day. Those who want to further their educations can use it as a stipend.
- It is paid out as one-third of total tax collections. If the government collects $3 trillion in taxes in a given year, then $1 trillion will be allocated for UBI. If there are 200,000,000 adults 18 or over in the country, then each adult receives $3 trillion / 200,000,000 = $15,000 per year to do with as you

please, whether you work or don't work. But no other forms of welfare are permitted.

Because the UBI is tied to tax collections, it will rise and fall with the economy, and will never put the government in deficit spending. It will remove the ability of Congress to waste money and bust budgets funding myriads of pet welfare programs that are more tailored to advancing the welfare bureaucracy's interests than the people's.

Corporate Responsibility

Corporations should grow their business the right way, by investing in new and improved goods and services that people want to buy. They should be discouraged from managing the wrong way, by firing the employees, bilking the cash flow into the Wall Street money funds' pockets, and steering the empty hulks into bankruptcy to void their pensions. I would suggest the following employee protections, for companies with over 500 employees or a billion dollars of publicly owned market cap.

- Layoffs must be a last resort. If a company permanently lays off more than 3% of its employees in a year, then the company must go through bankruptcy reorganization that wipes out the debt and cancels the stock. The creditors and stockholders must suffer along with the employees. Companies that lay their people off must be placed on a three-year prohibition in which no mergers or

148

acquisitions are allowed and the company cannot be sold to other owners; all executive contracts are voided; and maximum executive pay is capped at $500,000 a year, with no prospect of bonuses. Executives must never be rewarded for busting companies. Laid off employees must be rehired, if they request, before new people are brought into the company.

- Any "independent contractor" who works in the role of an employee, i.e. on the company's premises, using company equipment, and under company supervision, must be granted the option of becoming an employee, with all employee rights, including 401K contributions, backdated to the first day the "independent contractor" worked for the company. This will prevent companies from mis-classifying employees as contractors.

- Mergers and acquisitions must not create layoffs or defraud employees of their pension rights.

I also believe that if we're going to put companies in harness to serve the public interest, we should help them better serve the private interests of their stockholders. I've already mentioned eliminating unemployment insurance taxes. This is a very big deal. An even bigger one would be to shield companies from class action lawsuits. As in healthcare, there should be Public Service Commissions for each business group with professional adjudicators to hear product liability complaints fairly, with no interest in unjustly enriching attorneys.

Taxes, Spending, and the Debt Bomb

I believe in tax reform where it will "broaden the base and lower the rates," by removing tax shelters and unfair loopholes for special interests, but I do not see tax cuts as a panacea for economic growth.

Tax reform is necessary because our federal income tax was written in 1913 more to redistribute income that to fund the civil and military obligations of the national government. It was filled with deductions for state and local income taxes and charitable deductions. These deductions are meant to encourage state and local governments to raise taxes and for wealthy individuals to give away their money. It makes no sense to place the federal government, which has the most substantial obligations, at the back of the line for revenue, or to create situations where some people pay more federal income taxes on $100,000 of income than others pay on $10,000,000.

The tax code should be as "flat" as possible, with few deductions, and with rates the same for everybody. I believe Republicans did good work in capping the state and local tax deductions at $10,000. Now we should cap the charitable deductions at $10,000 and remove the exemptions for municipal bond income. That would send more money to the national government where it is needed to pay down ballooning debt. If

150

people want to donate to charities and buy municipal bonds, fine, but do it because your heart compels you, not because you're getting a tax deduction.

However, I do not buy Republican dogma that all tax cuts are beneficial. Some are, some aren't. Reagan's tax cuts certainly were, as they cut the top marginal rate from a confiscatory 70% to 28% and indexed the tax brackets to inflation. The Republican tax cuts of 2018 were also beneficial in my view, because they lowered rates and limited deductions, and made the United States more competitive for corporations. I think corporation executives whine too much about paying taxes and will never be happy with paying any taxes; they have even started demanding that cities and states subsidize them with other people's tax dollars. Nevertheless, this tax reduction took away their excuse for laundering tax dollars that should be paid on U.S. profits through tax havens like Ireland and the Channel Islands.

I also think that tax cuts are overblown as economic panaceas. The tax cuts occurring during George W. Bush's administration threw gasoline onto the fires of raging speculation and contributed to the economic conflagration of 2008. Bush should have been asking Congress to raise taxes to tamp down on the speculation, and to fund our global war on terror. The Bush tax cuts contributed to an economic collapse that had to be bailed out with even more government debt.

Democrats are able to claim, credibly in my view, that every dollar of tax cuts goes straight into increasing the federal debt, which will be a burden on our children and grandchildren. I don't think the Republican Establishment is going to get away with cutting taxes on big corporations and the wealthy while telling the middle class they'll have to forego their Social Security and Medicare. The Republican Establishment just got booted out of the House when their feckless leader Paul Ryan peddled that nonsense as "entitlement reform."

I don't believe reducing people's Social Security and Medicare is the correct way to constrain the debt bomb. The more Republicans talk about "entitlement reform," the quicker they will disappear as a major party. Republicans are as enthusiastic as Democrats about inviting Illegals into this country, whose healthcare is paid for by the government. Neither party is going to get way with denying healthcare to American citizens.

I would recommend raising tax revenues by:

- Capping charitable deductions at $10,000. Nobody should be able to shirk their tax burden by donating to dubious charities like The Home for Wayward Cats.
- Applying Social Security and Medicare taxes to all wages, and company-paid stock and stock option profits.
- Adding the Border Adjustment VAT of 20% * (USA revenues – USA cost inputs). Yes, I know nobody likes taxes, but we're going to have to pay them.

Better to require a fair tax on imports than to bust Americans' chops by raising taxes on people and products made in this country. Foreign-sourced products that extract profits from the United States should not be tax-advantaged over products produced in the United States by companies that invest here, hire here, produce here, and pay taxes here.

Green Energy and Climate Change

I am an "accidental" climate change analyst, having been coincidentally introduced to the subject in 1967 by the book **The Story of the Ice Age.** This book, which I still have, ends with a chapter called:

Danger Signs

There are signs that the Antarctic ice was thicker than now.....melting in the northern hemisphere might go on until the Artic Ocean again became free of ice Then there would be abundant evaporation from its surface, wetter air, and more snow. As a result, new ice sheets would probably form in North America, Europe, and Asia. The northern countries would be in danger [from ice]."

If this happens, we can be sure that nations will not sit idly by and let ice sheets overrun homelands....[we might cover] the surface with a dark material which would absorb more of the sun's heat. Or atomic reactors may be used to melt the ice.

153

Until now, man has adjusted to the ice. In the future, he may conquer it.

The book explained the comings and goings of the ice sheets as results of the Milankovitch Cycles that correlate the warming and cooling of the earth with astrophysical changes in its orbit and the tilt of the earth relative to the sun. The idea that Man's activities of emitting carbon into the air had anything to do with climate change were not widely discussed at that time.

This book isn't about climate change, so I'll only say that I've observed the climate in many parts of the world since becoming acquainted with the geophysical reasons for climate change. It was cold in the mid-60's through mid-80's, very warm in the 90's and early 2000's, and now is in between those extremes. Let's say there are three possibilities for climate change:

1. The climate isn't changing. It is just going through natural warming and cooling cycles before reverting to the norm.

2. The climate is changing modestly over a period of centuries, and Man probably has little or nothing to do with it, although it is impossible to know how much of the change is due to natural factors and how much is caused by Man.

3. The climate is changing rapidly, and Man is a primary cause.

I'm in the #2 camp. The very rapid increase in winter temperatures from around 1987 to 2005, followed by a return to record-breaking cold after 2013 makes me think Man is not causing the fluctuations. I know there are other opinions and that arguing about such a complex and emotion-laden subject isn't going to change anybody's mind. It's a political and emotional question, not a scientific one because climate has too many known and unknown variables to be analyzed according to the scientific method. Nevertheless, it is a political issue that must be addressed.

The important thing is to have a comprehensive plan and not attack it in dribs and drabs. There should be solar energy collectors in all areas that have sunny days to take the load off air conditioning. There should be wind farms where the wind blows often enough to be useful, which is not many places. We should use hydro, including buying it from Canada. We should do our part as citizens by buying electric vehicles. To gin up enough electricity to power electric vehicles, we are going to have to go massively nuclear.

The green energy people are going to have to accept nuclear power as the surest and quickest way to transition away from fossil fuels. The nuclear energy in a bomb the size of a short section of PVC pipe can destroy a city. We were making thousands of those devices each year during the Cold War. We can make these devices modular and safe, and put them to work powering cities by slow release of nuclear energy. We've got to do it if we want to get away from fossil fuels.

Infrastructure and Education

Democrats and even many Republicans love to spend money on "infrastructure and education". The roadbuilders, civil engineering companies, and education lobby loves that kind of spending too. Thus, there is always a hue and cry for spending on "our crumbling infrastructure and underfunded education."

I don't believe our infrastructure is crumbling. If it was, you wouldn't able to drive from Miami to Seattle or Boston to San Diego in a few days. If the infrastructure was crumbling the way the Infrastructure Mavens make it out to be, your tires would be shredded by potholes after thirty miles, and you'd take three months to cross the country on rutted dirt roads, after stopping to repair your car every other day. We haven't had roads like that in the United States since the 1800's. If the infrastructure were "crumbling" you wouldn't be flying in and out of airports that double as tony shopping malls and ritzy hotels.

The only places where the infrastructure is "crumbling" are in big cities where the tax money collected for roads and sewers is diverted to pay for bloated payrolls and pensions of municipal employees. Those burgs are bucking for a federal government bailout with "infrastructure" money that they will misappropriate in the same way they have misappropriated the money they already have.

Again, this is a political and emotional issue. I am sure that people whose meal tickets depend on state, local, and federal funding will continue to hoot about how the United States consists of nothing but dirt roads, bridges made of toothpicks, and one-room schools staffed with teachers who are paid with apples. So, throw some money their way, but not too much.

My Vote

The first political conversation I remember was during the 1964 election between Liberal Democrat Lyndon Johnson and Conservative Republican challenger Barry Goldwater. I was six years old. My father playfully asked me if I was a Democrat or a Republican. Not knowing anything at all about the parties other than their names, I answered "Democrat."

"It's best to vote for the best candidate, not the party," my father advised. He proved true to his word. He'd campaigned for Republican Richard Nixon in 1960 and would vote for him again in 1968 and 1972. However, in 1964 he voted for Liberal Democrat Lyndon Johnson. He always regretted that vote, because Johnsons' mismanagement of the Vietnam War proved catastrophic. He voted Democrat once more in 1976 when he lived in Georgia and voted for Jimmy Carter. He later regretted that vote too, but he felt that he had voted correctly based on the information available at the time.

I grew up with an outlook more conservative than my father's. I believe this outlook was genetically predisposed, because my parents didn't talk politics much and never sought to indoctrinate me with any political view. For whatever reasons, I grew up being a Conservative.

During my early 20's I never thought I'd ever vote for any Democrat. Now, decades, later I've done it twice. I voted for a Democratic neighbor in Chicago who is now the Secretary of

State of Illinois. I voted for and campaigned for Barack Obama in 2012. I'd donated to Mitt Romney's campaign in the Republican primaries, but as 2012 wore on, I came to see that Romney had been too much a part of the corrupt business practices that wrecked the economy in 2008. I felt Obama deserved to be re-elected and was pleased when he won.

My father occasionally spoke well of Democrats because he grew up during the Great Depression and felt that Franklin Roosevelt had saved the country. I understood why he felt that way after researching Progressive and New Deal agendas in my books *Five American Revolutions*, recently condensed into *The Diary of American Exceptionalism:*

https://www.amazon.com/Diary-American-Exceptionalism-Alan-Sewell-ebook/dp/B01H2HGCNC/

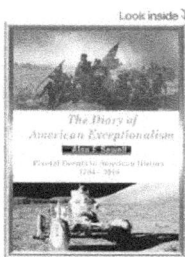

Look inside ↓

The Diary of American Exceptionalism: Pivotal Events in American History 1783 - 2019 Kindle Edition

by Alan Sewell - (Author)
Be the first to review this item

▸ See all formats and editions

Kindle
$0.00 kindleunlimited

Read with Kindle Unlimited to also enjoy access to over 1 million more titles
$8.50 to buy

"If we could first know where we are, and whither we are tending, we could better judge what to do, and how to do it."

So said Abraham Lincoln as he contemplated the great issues of containing slavery and preserving the Union. This book is written to show where we are, and whither we may be tending, by explaining our

Follow the Author

I came to understand how America's Progressives are correct on many economic issues. Franklin Roosevelt was wise to learn from them and courageous to implement them broadly in the 1930's. Republicans are also correct to warn that social welfare programs must not become so excessive as to become a permanent livelihood that discourages work.

Like most things in life, both Liberal / Progressive and Conservative / Populist agendas must be kept in balance and not taken to an extreme in either direction. However, they must not be so thoroughly diluted by establishment politicians as to lose all their effectiveness. We are now at another one of those turning points where we may need to sharpen the edges of Progressive Liberalism and Populist Conservativism, in order to get moving out of the rut that both parties' establishments have dug.

I, like many other Americans, was in a political funk toward the end of Obama's administration. I'd voted for Obama in 2012 despite feeling that he'd let the big business establishment water down his "change" agendas by 75%. By 2014 the country had substantially recovered from the calamities of 2008 but seemed unable to grow beyond that point. In 2014 I wrote Vice President Joe Biden, urging him to run in 2016, as I felt Ms. Clinton was too ethically-challenged and establishment-oriented to be elected. Biden is one of four prominent Democrats I've corresponded with. The others have been Bernie Sanders, Diane Feinstein, and my former Florida Senator Bill Nelson.

My correspondence with Bernie Sanders was in the early 2000s. He appeared on Larry Kudlow's CNBC show. Larry teased him a bit by calling him (paraphrasing) a "Socialist who doesn't represent anybody but yourself, and has no business coming on my show to insult my audience."

Bernie responded with a friendly laugh. "Now, Larry, you know I'm here, because you invited me. I represent the views of the people of Vermont who elected me." Larry laughed too, and they had a friendly exchange. I wrote Bernie, saying that I was impressed by his disarming response as well as his views. People admire politicians who have a little humility and don't take themselves too seriously. I liked that about Bernie and have had some affection for him ever since.

Senator Feinstein took time to respond to a business issue I wrote about from Illinois in the 1990's. She knew I wasn't a resident of California and would never vote for her, but she considered my opinion and put me on her mailing list, so I'd be aware of what she was doing about it. What a great Senator, to take time to thoughtfully respond to a letter from someone who could not vote for her! I was disappointed in her response to Brett Kavanaugh's nomination, but otherwise consider her to be fair-minded and thorough in examining all points of view about the issues. I mention her, Bernie Sanders, and Joe Biden to make it clear that many Trump voters, like me, are also willing to give Democrats a fair hearing. But if Democrats keep calling us "hicks, sexual predators, and racists" then our votes will default back to Trump and the Republicans.

I became a Trump backer when I heard him talk about reining in detrimental trade and immigration. I understand both issues from direct experience of running a multinational small business and being married into an immigrant family. I've lived and worked overseas. I see the detrimental effects of excessive trade and immigration, as well as the positives. The media, especially the business press, seeks to suppress the detrimental effects and thereby delude the public into supporting their view that trade and immigration are only ever beneficial. Like most other things, they are beneficial only up to a point, and are never beneficial when done with dishonest and illegal motives.

I was ambivalent about voting for Trump in the 2016 primaries, as he seemed to have become excessively rambunctious in mocking on the other candidates. An unexpected family emergency took me out of Florida on primary day, March 9, 2016, so I'll never know who I would have voted for, or if I would have even voted. Later, my support for Trump solidified. The more I saw him campaign, the more I realized that a lot of his personality was theatrical, and that solid common sense underlay most of his positions. I decided he was sincere in wanting to "make America great again," so I voted for him enthusiastically in the 2016 election.

An in-depth explanation of my voting Republican prior to 2012, voting for and campaigning for Obama in 2012, and voting for Populist Republican Trump in 2016 is explained by my review of *The Betrayal of the American Dream* by Donald L. Bartlett and James B. Steele. The book:

https://www.amazon.com/Betrayal-American-Dream-Donald-Barlett/dp/1586489690/

And the explanation of why I voted as I did in my review of it:

https://www.amazon.com/gp/customer-reviews/R2PG0XU0KGNA5R?ref=pf_vv_at_pdctrvw_srp

Now, in early April 2019, I am again ambivalent in my estimation of President Trump. He has succeeded in things he wasn't expected to --- such as working with Congressional Republicans to improve the tax code, appointing the best Conservatives to the federal courts, and defusing tense relations with North Korea. The economy, by most accounts, is on the mend, although the inequality issues I mentioned earlier remain sore spots.

On the other hand, he has failed to act on his pledges to balance the trade and secure the border. Both problems are more severe now than when he took office. His trade "deal" with China looks to be a sham, like all previous trade agreements have been. He has recently given Mexico "another year" to control their side of the border, which they are not capable of doing. In the meantime, record levels of illegal immigration will keep pouring into the country. Like Obama before him, Trump seems to have been neutered by the establishment wing of his party.

This is too bad, because the Republican Establishment was just booted out of the House in 2018. I expect them to lose the Senate in 2020. Like Obama, Trump is being led around by a party establishment that is being beaten in every election.

My vote in a year and a half is therefore undecided. Florida is not electing senators in 2020. I am pleased with my Republican Freedom Caucus congressman and have already decided to vote to re-elect him. I will only have to decide my vote for president, or to leave it blank if neither party nominates a candidate I can support.

As for Democrats, I consider their candidates Joe Biden, Elizabeth Warren, and Howard Schultz potentially worthy of my vote. I think Schultz is their best candidate who has so far announced. Like Bernie Sanders and Donald Trump, he is not part of the political Establishment. The Democratic Establishment may undermine his candidacy as they did Bernie Sanders, but the people may speak loud enough in the primaries to defeat the Establishments' anointed candidates. Elizabeth Warren, despite her soiree as an Indian, fits my views on the need to regulate business thoroughly, but not excessively. Joe Biden is a moderate Centrist, who I've already said I could vote for, but being a Centrist will harm him now that we're in a cycle where Centrists aren't popular.

So, as of April 2019, my vote in 2020 is undecided. It could be a split ticket where I vote for my Freedom Caucus congressman, while voting for the Democrat nominee for president. I would like to vote for Trump again, but he must give me reason to do it. As a 92-year-old spry businesswoman in a Florida town said the other day, "If he doesn't build the wall, we won't vote for him."

That, by the way, is why Democrats keep saying, "Walls don't work." Of course, walls work, that's why they're built everywhere. They just don't work for Democrats who are hoping to unseat Trump in 2020.

Prediction 2020

If the Fourth Turning theory is correct, then Donald Trump will either be the last of the Great Unravellers of the old post-WWII globalist order, or the progenitor of the new Populist / Nationalist 21st Century order.

My perspective is that people still feel that they were cheated out of the "change" that they were promised in 2008 and didn't get. People are still angry that the government only seems to work for the elite, well-connected, and well-to-do. Bankers got a bailout with government (taxpayer) money. Taxpayers lost their homes, jobs, businesses, and retirements. People are still angry about that. The definition of "change" that the people want is that the government is working for their interests, instead of those of crony capitalist banks and corporations, and the politicians they carry in their pockets. The Democrats are promising change from the Progressive Left. If the Republicans, led by Trump, can "out-change" them from the Populist Right, they will prevail. Otherwise, the country wants to shift toward the Progressive Left and restore at least an appearance of fairness from the government towards the wage-earning middle class.

The first decision for Trump is whether to seek re-election. Now, in April 2019, I believe he occupies the same position as President Obama did at a similar point in his term. He has worked with the Establishment Republicans in Congress to enact the Establishment's agendas, as Obama worked with Establishment Democrats. The economy is on the mend, as it was during most of Obama's presidency.

However, Trump has not yet addressed the significant issues of trade and immigration that got him elected. If he does not do so soon, time will pass him by, and he may fail of re-election. Failing to secure the border takes away the most prominent issue he campaigned on in 2016. He may lose the voters who voted for him primarily because of that issue. If he loses even 2% of the vote, he will fail of re-election, especially if the Democrats choose stronger, and less ethically-challenged, candidates in 2020 than in 2016. Trump may decide around November 2019 that his re-election situation is hopeless due to insurmountable opposition by the Republican and Democrat Establishments and much of the federal judiciary.

A counter-argument is that Trump is instinctively smart. He played the Mueller investigation optimally. He railed about it "being a witch hunt" but did nothing to disrupt it. He let the Democrats dig themselves into a deep hole by outrageously inflating their hopes that Mueller would indict Trump and his close associates and family of "Russian Collusion." The Democrats leaked false information to the press and made themselves look stupid and disreputable. He gave them enough rope to hang themselves.

He may yet do the same with trade and immigration. The Republican and Democrat Establishments keep telling us there is no border crisis. They have blocked Trump's efforts at border enforcement. He may let them have their way to the point where the United States is buried under tidal waves of illegal immigration. Then, when they have made fools of themselves, and have been discredited and voted out of office, he will enforce the border. He may do that, or he may join the Establishment in ignoring the problem. If he does that, then the Republicans and the country are headed for severe dysfunction. He likewise needs to reduce the skyrocketing trade deficit, especially with China, which hit another record high of $419 billion in 2018

https://www.census.gov/foreign-trade/balance/c5700.html

If Trump decides not to run again, I believe the Republican Establishment will nominate another Establishment candidate who will be crushed in a landslide. The Republicans' political consultants are quite capable of steering even their best candidates to defeat, by feeding them big-business agendas of {cutting taxes for the wealthy, making corporations tax-exempt charities; keeping the borders open to Chinese imports and people entering illegally from Central America; reducing Social Security and Medicare} that the people know are nonsense. Trump won in 2016 because he ignored the Republican Establishment's consultants and didn't let them anywhere near his campaign.

I expect the Democrats will nominate Senator Elizabeth Warren, who is a hybrid Establishment / Progressive candidate. I think she is skeptical enough of the banks and big business to represent the "change" that Obama felt would be too difficult to implement while we were still in the grip of the Great Recession. I think she will campaign on increasing regulation of business; modestly increasing taxes on the well-to-do; moving healthcare partially toward a single-payer system while leaving the private sector alone for people who want to continue receiving healthcare there; and raising the minimum wage. I believe it would be better for the Democrats to nominate Howard Schultz, but he will have to buck the party's Establishment. As Bernie Sanders found out, that will be difficult. The Democrats may also decide to come back to Joe Biden, if none of the new candidates catch fire.

I will go on the record as predicting the Democrats will nominate Senator Warren, although at the time of this writing, Bernie Sanders seems to be gaining ground. "Bernie's" (it is difficult to call him by anything other than his first name) strengths are that he is a political outsider, not even part of the Democratic Party until 2016; that he has not been corrupted by big banks and multinational corporations; that he articulates a Progressive agenda; that he is personable; and that he is not a bought-and-paid-for tool of either party's establishment.

I believe the Democrats' vice president will be an up-and-coming Progressive. That candidate will probably need to be white, male, and Midwestern to attract enough of that voting block to make an electoral majority. Mayor Pete Buttigieg of South Bend, Indiana is the current rising star (as of April 2019).

169

If for any reason he falters, the Democrats have other rising Congressmen, like Tim Ryan of Ohio, who fit the bill for a white male Midwesterner.

My prediction for Republicans is that Trump will decide, perhaps reluctantly, to run again, and that he will prevail by the same electoral vote majority as in 2016. I believe the Republicans will lose the Senate as voters reject their Establishment candidates. The election of 2020 will thus be a rerun of 2012 where a president who has accomplished 25% of what he promised, is nevertheless deemed worthy of re-election, even while the people reject his party's Establishment candidates in Congress.

If Trump loses and the Republicans lose the Senate, then maybe an all-Democrat government will do something constructive about healthcare, the minimum wage, and protecting employees from predatory corporate management. The Democrats can't be any worse about leaving the borders open to illegal immigration and trade deficits than the Republican Establishment already is.

In 2020, I will vote as my father advised me in 1964 "for the best candidate, and not for the party." I believe most Americans will do the same, and that the candidates who have the best view of the American people's interests will prevail.

Beyond 2020: The Reckoning

If the Cycles of History Theory is correct, the 2020 election will mark the consolidation of the United States under either the Republican Populist or Democratic Progressive tent. Will the crisis be over by then, or will it only be at its midpoint, with the most difficult days still to come as they were after the 1780, 1860, and 1940 turnings?

The 1940 Turning had the United States consolidated politically under Progressive Democrats, and the economy on the mend from the Great Depression, but there was still World War II to be fought. Let's hope there will be no more wars between major powers like the United States, Russia, and China. Wars often start small, and then spiral out of control catastrophically with deaths and destruction impossible to ever fully recover. So, let's hope all nations forsake war, now and forever.

What other crisis looms? The biggest one I can see is another Great Recession followed by the explosion of the Debt Bomb. The United States is currently adding to the national debt at the rate of a trillion a year and paying around $350 billion, nearly 10% of our annual federal budget, to paying interest on the debt. That's during a time of relative prosperity. If the economy tanks again, the deficit will soar exponentially.

We were able to float our way out of the Great Recession by issuing trillions of new government debt. We may not be able to do that again. We may have to conjure the money out of thin air, resulting in hyperinflation and unpredictable consequences for business. We might be able to work our way through it, or it might set our standard of living back a century. In chaotic times of hyperinflation, countries often disintegrate into warring factions, each trying by desperate means to protect the little it has left. If this happens to the United States, as it has happened to every other great power, then our role as a global power is finished. The Chinese will inherit the world. They are trying to expedite that day by weakening the United States with trade deficits and theft of our intellectual capital. I hope our disintegration into irrelevance does not happen, but history suggests that it might. Thus, our existential crises may only be just beginning. It may follow the political realignment of 2020.

A happier post-2020 outcome would be for the country to consolidate around the Republican Populists or Democrat Progressives, and we enter another "An Era of Good Feelings" --- reminiscent of the period that followed the dissolution of the Federalist Party after the War of 1812, and the reuniting of the country around Thomas Jefferson's and James Madison's Democratic-Republicans. An era of political rancor that nearly led to an early civil war became an era of renewal and expansion. Which ever party prevails, it will be the duty of the opposition to make their peace with it.

If the Populist Republicans prevail, the economy will take on more of a nationalist character, with the encouragement of the return of manufacturing. Globalization will not be eliminated, but it will be pared back about 30%, and the mania to remove all American jobs overseas so that the corporation 1% can hog the assets of the country will be restrained.

If the Progressive Democrats prevail, the country will take on the character of the New Deal and Great Society. Government and business will become partners, with government being the CEO and big business being the Executive Vice President. This will align the United States with the state-sponsored economies in Europe, Japan, China, and South Korea. Taxes may go back up to 70%, but fewer people will be left out of the economy. Employers will be encouraged to exercise more social responsibility to their employees and to the nation.

Voices of Hope

We are living in a polarized political time. The Democrats have acted like petulant children ever since Trump was elected, just as the Republicans did when Obama was elected in 2008 and 2012. They have invented preposterous charges of "Russian Collusion," and leaked false information to the media, which has reported the misinformation without conscience. Liberal "comedians" tell jokes about Trump on national television that are more prurient than I ever heard in junior high school. Then again, Trump's persona is not the epitome of maturity and calm judgment.

The Republicans also went overboard when Democrats were in the White House. The Republican Whitewater prosecutions of Bill Clinton could have been handled in the civil courts instead of as an Act of Congress. That investigation damaged Bill Clinton, although he brought a lot of it on himself, and sullied Ms. Clinton's reputation, justifiably perhaps, to the point where she became un-electable. The Republicans' "birther" rumors about Obama being born outside the United States were offensive. So, it is no surprise that the Democrats were primed for vengeance when Trump was elected. Trump has certainly done his share of baiting them. Let's just say that both sides need to tone it down.

Let's also remember that political animosity is nothing new. Democracies, where people can speak their minds, often to excess, are rarely civil. Even George Washington was stung by partisan attacks while he was president:

Until within the last year or two ago, I had no conception that parties would or even could go to the lengths I have been witness to, nor did I believe until lately that it was within the bounds of probability; hardly within those of possibility, that while I was using my utmost exertions to establish a national character of our own, to preserve this country from the horrors of a desolating war, that I should be accused of being the enemy of one nation [France] and subject to the influence of another [Britain], and every act of my administration should be tortured and the grossest and most insidious misrepresentations of them be made, and that in such exaggerated and indecent terms as could scarcely be applied to a Nero, a notorious defaulter, or even to a common pickpocket.

Let's also not forget that Americans of all political stripes have a common destiny greater than the sum of our political divisions. As John Adams said in 1765:

I always consider the settlement of America with reverence and wonder, as the opening of a grand scene, and design in Providence, for the illumination of the ignorant and the emancipation of the slavish part of Mankind all over the earth.

After winning our Independence, George Washington frequently doubted whether Americans would be able to put aside their petty squabbles and local jealousies long enough to fulfill that destiny:

The citizens of America, as sole lords and proprietors of a vast tract of continent, are the actors on a most conspicuous theater which seems to be peculiarly designated by Providence for the display of human greatness and felicity. It is in their choice whether they will be respectable and prosperous, or contemptible and miserable, as a nation. For according to the system of policy the states shall adopt at this moment, they will stand or fall, and by their confirmation or lapse, it is yet to be decided whether the Revolution must ultimately be considered as a blessing or a curse, not to the present age alone, for with our fate will the destiny of unborn millions be involved.

Americans have the power to become one of the most respectable nations on earth, if we could but pursue a wise, just, and liberal policy towards one another. But my fear is that the people are not yet sufficiently mislead to retract from error.

Washington urged reconciliation between Alexander Hamilton and Thomas Jefferson when partisan rancor and sectional animosities threatened to fragment the United States in the 1790s:

Mankind cannot think alike but would adopt different means to attain the same end. For I will frankly, and solemnly declare that, I believe the views of both of you are pure, and well meant...

Nearly a century and a half later, during the economic distress of the Great Depression, Franklin Roosevelt reminded us that even in the midst of economic and political distress, when

176

clamor for radical change is highest, that we must look first toward preserving our founding principles:

Say that civilization is a tree which, as it grows, continually produces rot and dead wood. The Radical says: Cut it down. The Conservative says: Don't touch it. The Liberal compromises: Let's prune, so that we lose neither the old trunk nor the new branches.

And finally, let's remember Mr. Lincoln's patient restraint during the Civil War when he was provoked by criticism from all sides. In 1862 newspaper editor Horace Greeley published an inflammatory editorial telling Mr. Lincoln that Northerners "are sorely disappointed and deeply pained by the policy you seem to be pursuing......the world will lay the blame on you. Whether you will choose to hear it through future History and 'at the bar of God,' I will not judge."

Rather than replying in anger, Mr. Lincoln responded with calm understanding:

*I have just read yours of the 19th. addressed to myself through the **New-York Tribune**.*

If there be in it any statements, or assumptions of fact, which I may know to be erroneous, I do not, now and here, controvert them.

If there be in it any inferences which I may believe to be falsely drawn, I do not now and here, argue against them.

If there be perceptible in it an impatient and dictatorial tone, I waive it in deference to an old friend, whose heart I have always supposed to be right.

Like Mr. Lincoln, let us think of our fellow Americans citizens as old friends, who, though sometimes intemperate, have hearts that are right. If we think that way toward our fellow Americans, all will yet be well.

About the Author

"Understanding history is a key to understanding the present and extrapolating the future."

- Alan Sewell

I've devoted my life to analyzing historical and current events and applying their historical lessons to today's business and economic issues. Although every day is a new day, the new days are layered on top of repeating cycles of history as old as Mankind. The more we understand the cycles of history, the more complete will be our understanding of the present.

I am an author and former business owner of companies operating in the USA, Canada, Europe, South America, and Asia Pacific. My other books are:

https://www.amazon.com/Alan-Sewell/e/B00557PQDY

My book ***The Diary of American Exceptionalism*** is an analysis of prior pivot points in American History, from the American Revolution to the present:

https://www.amazon.com/Diary-American-Exceptionalism-Alan-Sewell-ebook/dp/B01H2HGCNC/

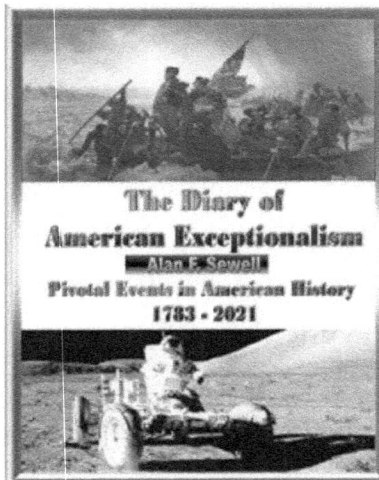

"If we could first know where we are, and whither we are tending, we could better judge what to do, and how to do it."

So said Abraham Lincoln as he contemplated the great issues of containing slavery and preserving the Union. This book is written to show where we are, and whither we may be tending, by explaining our current political controversies in the context of where we have been at similar crisis points in the past.

As this book is being updated for the 2021 Edition, the controversies have intensified beyond what most Americans would have believed possible. Yet we remain the essential, exceptional nation, a continent-wide republic of ambitious and outspoken free people. This book is written as a distilled essence of American history, explained in the words of the people who made it. It focuses narrowly but intensively on six periods of quantum change that moved us into new political and economic directions. Since it appears that we may be at another turning point in our history, it may provide insights into our future direction.

I also admire Abraham Lincoln's principled and patient leadership. I have written **August 23, 1864: The Day that Abraham Lincoln won the Civil War**:

https://www.amazon.com/August-23-1864-Abraham-Lincoln/dp/0997226889

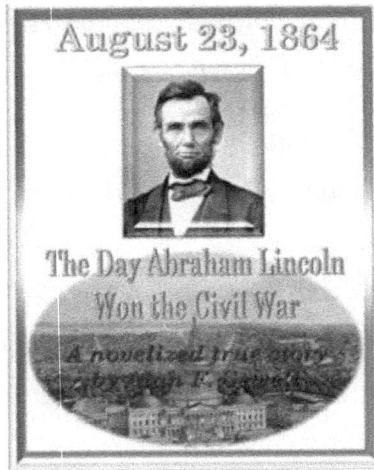

August 23, 1864

The Day Abraham Lincoln
Won the Civil War

A novelized true story

Abraham Lincoln began the morning of August 23, 1864 by despairing of re-election:

"This morning, as for some days past, it seems exceedingly probable that this Administration will not be re-elected. Then it will be my duty to so co-operate with the President elect (George McClellan, running on the Peace Platform), as to save the Union between the election and the inauguration; as he will have secured his election on such ground that he cannot possibly save it afterwards."

The Union was losing as many as 15,000 men killed, crippled, and dead from disease per week. Men up to the age of 45 were being conscripted to fill the gaping holes. Many deserted or surrendered at the first opportunity. Officers who had turned Lee back at Gettysburg last year had been killed or discharged with wounds. Incompetents and drunkards took their places. Grant's army was suffering staggering defeats at battles it would have

182

won in previous years. On August 23rd bad news poured in from all fronts. Lincoln's friends warned him he would not be re-elected. George McClellan, a pre-war protege of Jefferson Davis, would be the next president.

During the course of the day, Mr. Lincoln made a series of decisions that swung the balance back in his favor and enabled him to prevail in November's election, thus seeing the war through to Union victory.

Please address feedback to: alsnewideas@gmail.com